Proud to Work

A Pictorial History of Michigan's Civilian Conservation Corps

Annick Hivert Carthew

Wilderness Adventure Books

ISBN: 0-923568-73-5

Cover photo credits: Front cover, clockwise from top, photos courtesy of Douglas Key Renny (photos 1, 3, 4), Newaygo County Society of History and Genealogy (photo 2); Back cover, top to bottom, photos courtesy of Douglas Key Renny, Michelle Kuffer, Newaygo County Society of History and Genealogy

Library of Congress Cataloging-in-Publication Data

Hivert-Carthew, Annick.

   Proud to work : Michigan's Civilian Conservation Corps / Annick Hivert Carthew.

      p. cm.

   Includes bibliographical references (p.   ) and index.

   ISBN 0-923568-73-5

   1. Civilian Conservation Corps (U.S.)–Michigan–History. 2. Conservation of natural resources–Michigan–History. 3. Civilian Conservation Corps (U.S.)–Michigan–Pictorial works. 4. Conservation of natural resources–Michigan–Pictorial works. I. Title.

   S932.M4C37 2006

   333.75'1609774–dc22

                                        2006001399

Contents

Acknowledgments

First of all, I would like to thank all the CCC alumni who penetrated Michigan's unforgiving wilderness to reshape our landscape. You have labored unstintingly to leave a wonderful legacy for generations after generations. For this, we are very grateful.

This book would not have been possible without the help and cooperation of numerous people who gave their time and effort to this project, especially Dale Herder Ph.D., Professor of English and Emeritus Vice President, Lansing Community College, Chair, Michigan Bring Back the CCC Committee, and Frank Munger, CCC veteran, who offered their support and knowledge and were kind enough to participate in the writing of this book. Loren Estleman, author of the Amos Walker Detroit mystery series; Patrick J. McKay, Museum Director, Rochester Hills Museum at Van Hoosen Farm; Dr. Dale Herder (again), Susan Whitall of the *Detroit News*, thank you for taking time off from your busy schedule to review this book.

To the many 1933-1942 CCC veterans, friends and kin who shared their memories, life and achievements—Don Ashcroft, Leo Lamar Athey, Marvin Bond, Rainelle Burton, Bonner Burton, Henry Renny, Douglas Key Renny, Charles Crafard, Clark Curry, Arthur Barnes, Marvin Bond, Diana Dinverno, Robert Elmer Dodge, Reverend William Elum, Betty Edwards, Doris Fedus, Waldo "Red" Fisher, James Fournier, Robert Fyvie, John Gilmour, Cameron Glynn, Wayne and Dorothy Hamilton, Edward Hartzell, Antoine Jackson, Ray Larson, Elmer Leach, Gerald McNeil, Bernard McGill, Frank Munger, Gerard Perry, "Philipps," Michael Rataj, John Selesky, Clarence Springer, Anne Thatcher, Wells Hall, William Tylutki, Stan Ward, Josephine Smalligan Wharff, Donovan Dean Wharff, Walter Wildey, George Yannett—I offer my deep appreciation; talking to you was an honor and immense pleasure.

I am especially indebted to Frank Munger, Michael Rataj, Leo Lamar Athey, posthumously Douglas Key Renny, the Douglas Craig Renny Family, Ray Larson, and Robert Dodge who generously loaned their never-published collections of pictures.

Thanks are also due to contributors who went out of their way to provide additional information: Rob Burg, Site Historian, Logging Museum, CCC Museum & Tawas Point Lighthouse; Dick Armstrong, docent at CCC Museum; William Jamerson, author of documentary "Camp Forgotten"; Professors Carolyn Gillespie and Laura Friesen and Dr. Lauren Friesen, from University of Michigan-Flint; Rosemary Michelin from Marquette County Historical Society; Sandy Vincent from Fremont Area District Library; Hank Bailey; Annette Kingsbury from the *Rochester Eccentric*; and LuAnn Zettle from West Branch Centennial Committee.

Vanderbilt Residential Camp

Josh Cline, I am so grateful you answered my Internet CCC quest and put me in touch with your fellow alumni. Emily Peck, what would I have done without you? Keep going, girl, you will inspire many women to reach for the stars.

A big thank you to the men and women of Vanderbilt Camp; you have been fantastic and are a treasure to this country; David Turner, Michelle Kuffer, Kasha Kuznicki, Timothy J. Ruhlman, Kristopher and Kelly Carpenter, Matt Fink, Thomas Miller, Gene Withers, Joe and Crystal Venohr, Robert Brown, and Calvin Houghton. I loved meeting all of you at the Upper Cabin.

Hartwick Pine, Sign Shop

Robert C. Studer, Parks and Recreation Supervisor 9, thank you for your warm hospitality and for giving me time to interview your team. Young people, Jennifer Marie Failing, Mary Louise Racine, Jenna McClain, Alex Chase, Chris Nelson, Billy Murphy, and Sarah Jones; it was so much fun meeting you at the CCC Museum in Roscommon. I enjoyed your liveliness, good sense of humor and friendliness.

Iris Underwood and Mira Stephaniuk; it's wonderful to have your support.

Erin Sims Howarth, from Wilderness Adventure Books, it is so nice to be working with you again. This project required lots of patience and creativity, both of which you have. Thank you.

Julie Wallis, I promise "no more scanning" for a while. Your kindness is appreciated.

My dear family, you've listened to my CCC stories month after month without complaining, and conducted interviews in 97° F weather; this book belongs to you too. Your support and love are vital to my success.

To the "Bring Back the CCC" Committee, I wish you luck with this worthy cause.

To the countless others, too numerous to cite here, please accept a big heartfelt appreciation.

Foreword

The astounding success of the CCC in the 1930s and 1940s begs a question: If the CCC was so good seventy years ago, why don't we bring it back today?

As the national and Michigan Chairman of the Bring Back the CCC Committee, I believe the words "Bring Back the CCC" are much easier to say than they are to put into ACTION. Talk is cheap. Action requires things that are not always easy to find: Leadership, commitment, teamwork, political support, infrastructure, funding, follow-through.

In 1992-93, I spent a year on sabbatical leave to study and lecture about democracy and to revitalize the CCC in the United States. I was convinced that the U.S. needed a form of voluntary community service similar to the mandatory service required in many other nations. I traveled extensively on a lecture and research tour that took me around the world, and I spent six months working with Lloyd Mielke, Bill Fraser, Frank Munger, John Roundtree, and the Board of Directors of the National Association of CCC Alumni (NACCCA) to help bring back the CCC. The project was to become a commitment for the entire next decade.

In 1993, while meeting in St. Louis with the NACCCA Board, I suggested a national rally of CCC alumni in Washington to gain the support of the Clinton Administration. President Lloyd Mielke and the NACCCA Board of Directors liked the idea. President Clinton responded favorably to the rally and the efforts of NACCCA, and shortly thereafter he made a series of speeches and presentations in which he spoke highly about the CCC and the wisdom of President Franklin D. Roosevelt for establishing the Cs in 1933. In the months following the rally, national figures such as Robert Dole, Leon Panetta, Larry King, Paul Harvey, Daniel Patrick Moynihan, and Newt Gingrich spoke out favorably about bringing back the CCC.

After over 300 phone calls to congressional representatives and a trip to Washington to meet with President Clinton's staff (including an especially positive meeting with Mr. Leon Panetta, Director of the U.S. Budget), a "Bring Back the CCC Rally" was held on the front steps of the U.S. Capitol on July 16, 1993. CNN provided nationwide coverage for three days.

Unfortunately for the effort to resurrect a national CCC, President Clinton and the U.S. Congress had already committed money and established jobs for people who were to lead AmeriCorps. The politics and funding were in place, and there was no way to undo them in order to bring back FDR's vision in the 1990s.

Undaunted, the NACCCA team adopted a motto ("There is nothing so powerful as an idea whose time has come—again!") and told its chapters around the U.S. that it would be up to them to organize their own committees, contact their own state governors, and work with their own state legislatures to build camps in as many states as possible. California, Ohio, and Michigan were especially successful. Reverend Bill Fraser and Frank Munger, two former CCC "boys" who had successfully established the Michigan CCC Museum and organized annual Michigan reunions of CCC alumni, pulled together a team that agreed to lead the Michigan's effort to establish residential CCC camps. The Michigan Bring Back the CCC Committee was comprised of William Fraser, Dale Herder, William Jamerson, Ron Joyce, Arthur Kerle, Richard Laing, Hertha Laupmanis, Kenneth Mortenson, Frank Munger, and John Selesky.

The Michigan Committee planned a multi-faceted strategy and got busy. It worked positively with both sides of the political aisle in the Michigan legislature, and it achieved the support of both Governor James Blanchard (a Democrat) and his successor, Governor John Engler (a Republican). The Committee also identified two "champions" in the Michigan House and Senate whose leadership and seniority made it possible for the Department of Natural Resources (DNR) to receive appropriations so it could establish three new residential CCC camps. The first was in the Northern Lower Peninsula (Camp Vanderbilt), the second was in the Upper Peninsula (Camp Alberta), and the third was in the Southern Lower Peninsula (Camp Proud Lake).

The two legislative "champions" who worked hand-in-glove with the Michigan Bring Back the CCC Committee and the Michigan Department of Natural Resources were Democratic Representative Thomas Mathieu (the "father" of the revitalized CCC in Michigan) and Republican Senator George McManus. Both men held a deep personal conviction that CCC camps could do wonders for Michigan's natural environment—and for the unemployed youth of Michigan. They were right.

Even though Michigan's senior DNR professional staff sought to invest in NON-resident CCC projects in order to stretch the DNR budget as far as possible, Mr. Steve Philip and Mr. Ross Dodge (the DNR administrators who were responsible for Michigan's CCC) were able to strike a miraculous balance between the Bring Back the CCC Committee, their offices, the legislature, and their bosses. They made sure that as many young CCC enrollees as possible were living in camps, just as their predecessors had seventy years before. The national CCC alumni and the Michigan CCC alumni were unanimous in their insistence that CCC enrollees LIVE IN CAMPS, in order to break away from the toxic influences that permeated their neighborhoods and homes. The experience of three million boys in the 1930s and 1940s was powerfully compelling: It had taught them that young people can become proud and responsible citizens in our democracy if they have good role models and know the power of teamwork in order to accomplish a goal that advances the common good.

All three Michigan camps now are closed because of budget constraints, but the Michigan Bring Back the CCC Committee still is alive and well. When the economic winds blow more favorably, it is hoped that Camp Alberta will be the first to re-open, with the support of the legislature, the Governor, and Michigan Technical University, which owns the property where Camp Alberta is located in Michigan's Upper Peninsula.

Nothing is so powerful as an idea whose time has come—again!

—Dale M. Herder Ph.D., Chair, Bring Back the CCC Committee.

By the time the Michigan economy went into the doldrums after the stock market high-tech crash at the end of the 1990s, hundreds of Michigan youth had been served magnificently by their experience of living together, working hard, learning a lot, and earning a little.

FDR with CCC recruits.

Michigan "Soil Soldiers" Serve Their Country

102,000 young Michigan men answer President F. D. Roosevelt's call

The year was 1933. They were young men between the age of eighteen and twenty-five. Unemployed, poor, hungry, and "idle through no fault of their own,"[1] their morale had sunk to an all-time low.

[1] President Franklin Delano Roosevelt

A dark cloud hung over America. The prosperity of the "Roaring Twenties" had ended with a bang in 1929 when the New York Stock Exchange crashed, provoking an economic chaos that wrought endless misery to the masses of people who lost jobs, homes, and pride.

Then one presidential candidate with the theme song "Happy Days are Here Again," pledged to the American people to create work programs as part of a "New Deal" if they elected him.

Within a month of his inauguration on March 4, 1933, Democrat Franklin Delano Roosevelt implemented his brainchild and pet project, specifically designed for jobless young men as part of the series of work programs he had promised: the Civilian Conservation Corps (CCC). The CCC aimed to engage unemployed youth in the "prevention of forest fires, floods, and soil erosion, plant, pest and disease control." The CCC included all races and ethnic groups, African Americans, Native Americans, but whites

"Happy Days are here again
The skies above are clear again
So let's sing a song of cheers again
Happy days are here again..."

Newaygo Camp

composed the bulk of the enrollees. Roosevelt declared that the CCC would "pay dividends to the present and future generations…"

It did—all over the U.S. and even more so in Michigan, where over 102,000 young men, distributed over 130 camps, answered the call between 1933 and 1942.

Michigan's CCC enrollees led the nation in planting 485 million trees, building forest fire towers, 7,000 miles of truck trails, 504 bridges, and 222 buildings. They established state parks and camping areas, erected dams, cleaned up rivers and improved habitat for fish and fowl, and planted more fish than any other state. They also spent 140,000 days fighting forest fires.

Armed with plain shovels and dressed in scratchy WWI

Before work, looking neat in recycled WWI uniforms.

leftover uniforms, they penetrated Michigan's unforgiving wilderness to reshape the American landscape for future generations.

Several famous men toiled in the CCC in their youth, such as Frank Sinatra, Joe Louis, Robert Mitchum, Marlon Brando, Walter Matthau, and Raymond Burr.

In 1942, with the entry of America in WWII, the CCC was discontinued. Many of its veterans volunteered in the armed forces and, according to their leaders, made the finest soldiers.

This is the story of the Michigan Civilian Conservation Corps "boys" and their day-to-day lives and achievements.

courtesy of Douglas Key Renny

"Strong backs, digging a gravel pit with shovels, one scoop at a time" at Camp Irons in 1936.

courtesy of Douglas Key Renny

Trout stream improvement on Little Manistee River, East of Peacock, off M63. Summer of 1935.

Leo Lamar Athey standing in front of a tent.

courtesy of Leo Lamar Athey

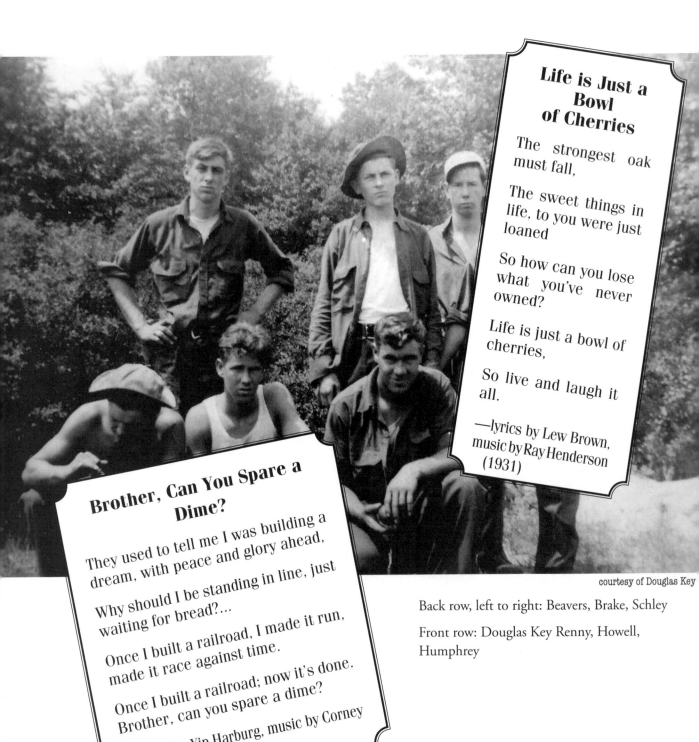

Life is Just a Bowl of Cherries

The strongest oak must fall,

The sweet things in life, to you were just loaned

So how can you lose what you've never owned?

Life is just a bowl of cherries,

So live and laugh it all.

—lyrics by Lew Brown, music by Ray Henderson (1931)

Brother, Can You Spare a Dime?

They used to tell me I was building a dream, with peace and glory ahead,

Why should I be standing in line, just waiting for bread?...

Once I built a railroad, I made it run, made it race against time.

Once I built a railroad; now it's done. Brother, can you spare a dime?

—lyrics by Yip Harburg, music by Corney Harburg (1931)

courtesy of Douglas Key

Back row, left to right: Beavers, Brake, Schley

Front row: Douglas Key Renny, Howell, Humphrey

Investing in Human Capital

"Our Greatest task is to put people to work." —President Franklin Roosevelt, 4 March, 1933

The American dream of lasting prosperity—listening to the radio, talking on the telephone, and driving an automobile—had come to an abrupt end in 1929. The Great Depression had set in. Prior to it, and for the first time in history, workers had had a bit of money left over to invest in the stock market, something previously affordable only to the rich.

When the stock market collapsed, so did the nation's economy. Many people lost their jobs, money, and homes. Farmers, unable to pay their mortgages, faced foreclosure. Nobody escaped. Previously financially-secure Americans discovered the meaning of abject poverty; they stood in frayed clothes in soup lines side by side with the poor.

Men who had supported their families with decent jobs begged for spare change and scraps of food. Families broke down. Hungry young people dropped out of school and hopped on trains in search of a better future or joined gangs of hopeless youths on the prowl.

The Nation faced formidable challenges. The future was uncertain and morale was low. Popular songs re-

"My grandmother, a widow with five children, was so poor that one day she opened one tin of meat from the government, lined up her children against a wall, opened the tin and gave each child a spoonful. That was supper."

—Diana Dinverno

"My uncle worked all over for farmers and anywhere else he could get a job to support our family. We picked berries and hunted hares."
—Betty Edwards, Grand Traverse Band of Chippewa and Ottawa Indians

flected the morale of the country. In 1932, "Brother Can You Spare a Dime," was sung at every street corner and Will Rogers quipped on the radio, "We're the first nation in the world to go to the poor house in an automobile."

Early every morning, factories threw a few shovels at anxious masses of men pressing against their gates. Whoever caught a shovel had work for the day. Single men were excluded from the melee; they did not have a wife and children to support.

Prosperity shattered and business at a stand-still, people endeavored to survive as best they could.

George Yannett, an Odawa from the Grand Traverse Band, commented that, "When I was in the CCC, I rarely went home; why should I go home to depend on my folk when they had nothing?"

Josephine Smalligan Wharff's parents were farmers. "Chicken feed was delivered in big mash sacks. Mother took them apart and washed them. Plain sacks were used for petticoats, dishtowels, tablecloths and pillow cases. Sometimes she embroidered the edges to make them look prettier. It took several bags to create one linen. Printed sacks were reserved for dresses and apron. Mother also saved fat from pork and mixed it with lye to make soap."

Antoine Jackson, Grand Traverse Band of Chippewa and Ottawa Indians
courtesy of Betty Edwards

"My father had a two-year college education, but had to hide it in order to get a job at Bud Wheels. Employers and coworkers alike mistrusted a guy with education, especially if he was black. They suspected him of being a trouble maker, arousing other people to rebel, and if the job was beneath him, not to apply himself to it."
—Rainelle Burton

Ingenuity reigned, and the Smalligan family saved money by substituting Ryzon for more expensive food items like eggs and reusing bags of sugar and feed.

Through ingenuity, Josephine's family fared quite well compared to others. Her husband, Donovan Dean Wharff, endured tougher times. He lived in the country. "Mother took in ironing from a storekeeper. Every day she walked two miles to a farmhouse to take care of a bedridden lady with two sons. She cooked and cleaned their house for twenty-five cents a day. I was twelve when we moved to Pontiac for Father's new job in a foundry at Pontiac Motors. Until then, I had never been in a city and had attended a one-room school and was scared to death to change classes at my new large school."

"I saw family after family in little red wagons trucking up and down the streets, scrounging for whatever they could find."
—Waldo "Red" Fisher

Some people reported never having tasted candy. Others recall eating a handful of crumbled, dampened flour

Josephine Smalligan Wharff wearing an apron made by her mother out of feed sacks.

thrown into a pan of sizzling lard for breakfast, lunch and dinner. Hobos jumped off trains at places where other hobos had planted signs indicating that the owner of the land was willing to feed them in exchange for work. Others, having lost everything, lived in cardboard shacks and lined up at soup kitchens.

Many of the future CCC recruits fared badly.

"My father had died, Mother worked in a factory, I had too much time on my hands and was getting in a lot of trouble." Don Ashcroft, CCC veteran

"I worked for a pittance wherever I could." Charles Crafard, CCC veteran

"I did not have a bike until I was sixteen." Wayne Hamilton, CCC veteran

"My dad made me pick up cigar butts to put in his pipe." William Tylutki, CCC veteran

It is not surprising that Franklin Delano Roosevelt based his 1932 presidential campaign on finding solutions to the Great Depression that gripped this country, especially by creating productive employment. After his election, he declared on 4 March, 1933, that "Our greatest task is to put people to work."

FDR was especially concerned about the possible waste of a whole generation of unemployed young men—the future of America—rapidly falling through the cracks of society. Undernourished, in tattered clothes, idle, and desperate, some of these youths had begun stealing and fighting, further endangering the crumbling safety of their neighborhoods.

An ardent conservationist, Roosevelt's intent with the Civilian Conservation Corps

"A guy I played baseball with came home one evening to papers spread on the kitchen table.
'Sign these,' his mother said, handing him a pen.
'What's this?' he asked.
'CCC enrollment papers.'
'I'm not joining the CCC.'
'Nobody asked your opinion. You're going.'
And he went."

—Michael Rataj

(CCC) was to employ "at risk" male youth and restore their pride and morale and to mend damage done to millions of deforested acres of American landscape by uncontrolled timber harvesting, soil erosion, and fire. With this program, Roosevelt "brought together two wasted resources, the young men and the land, in an effort to save both."[1] FDR's Civilian Conservation Corps program attracted many of these young men, and if it did not, it appealed to their parents, the local policemen, and clergy who witnessed their morale decline. A few mothers made their sons sign on the dotted line of application papers.

[1] NACCA, **"A Brief History of the Civilian Conservation Corps"**

Camp Harrison Retreat.

courtesy of Douglas Key Renny

"To give you an idea what twenty-five dollars could buy then, when my parents received my first pay, they borrowed my brother's old car, and put enough gas in it to drive to the nearest warehouse. They purchased $22.83 worth of goods. They loaded the car so much that my father had to walk home! We were so hungry that we would have worked just for food. Most of the boys put on between six and twenty-five pounds within the first few months at camp."

—Michael Rataj

courtesy of Douglas Key Renny

Richard Raupp. The CCC stopped the ache of empty bellies and lifted broken spirits. The boys were so happy that $25/month went to their families.

courtesy of Douglas Key Renny

Dump Drivers, July '36. 100^0 F. Boy is it hot! CCC boys worked in deep snow, slippery ice, and torrid weather day in and day out.

The Greatest Program

"I pledge you, I pledge myself to a new deal for the American people."
—Franklin Delano Roosevelt

When the CCC was instituted as unemployment relief, nearly a quarter of American workers were out of work. The CCC program alone would employ over three million young men nationwide. Among the New Deals, "The most popular program was the Civilian Conservation Corps," wrote Thomas Thurston, regional director, Building America: The Public Works of the New Deal Era.

The "boys" had to be unemployed, between the age of eighteen and twenty-five, single, from cities and farms, U.S. citizens, and coming from families on assistance. According to the *Forestry News Digest's* promotional article, young men had to be rescued from "city streets, have poor food, insufficient clothing and unventilated and unsanitary living quarters."

The average Michigan CCC enrollee applied willingly at a local selection board or was sometime dragged there by the authority or a parent in the hopes of "straightening him out."

"By 1937, it was hard to get in; many mothers, seeing neat, disciplined and polite boys coming back from camps, wanted their sons to be part of the program." Michael Rataj

courtesy of Douglas Key Renny

Ed Schultz standing straight, neat, and disciplined.

The boy had to be judged capable of hard physical labor, be out of school (many had not finished eighth grade), stand between 5 and 6.5 feet tall and weigh at least 107 pounds. During the initial physical examination, sympathetic doctors wiggled these seemingly strict requirements to let in needy applicants with borderline physical characteristics.

"An applicant was 1.5 pounds too light. Doc handed him a full pitcher of water and said, 'Go and drink it all. Come back when you're done.' He did, passed the weight regulation, and rushed to pee." Michael Rataj

Specific height and weight were not the only requirements. Applicants with varicose veins, venereal disease, or having less than three "serviceable masticating teeth above and below" were dismissed and transported home.

Enrollees were to work five days a week, be clothed, fed and housed, and receive one dollar a day or thirty dollars a month (room and board included), twenty-five of which were automatically sent to their dependents who received

"Once you got into camp, you wanted to get home, but after receiving a letter from your family who received twenty-five dollars and told you what they had been able to purchase with that money—a coat, food, and wood for the stove—you felt for the first time that you were helping your family and nothing could induce you to leave the CCC."

—Michael Rataj

a card stating that, "Allotment check will be mailed to you on or about the 10th of each month. Do not telephone or write in regard to check until after that date."

Enrollees spent their remaining five dollars at the camp canteen and the nearby community. The government put the twenty-five dollars of enrollees without dependents in a government saving account that they could cash when being discharged.

Robert Fechner, a former Machinist Union official from Boston, headed the program. Upon his death in 1939, his assistant, James J. McEntee, assumed the directorship.

Four departments—Labor, Agriculture, Interior, and the Army—composed the Advisory Council. A budget director was given the task to provide the necessary funds.

courtesy of Leo Lamar Athey

Leo Lamar Athey posing for the camera, "Look Mom, I've made it!"

According to the department's guidelines, the Corps was reserved for men only. Troubled by the similar plight of unemployed women, Eleanor Roosevelt pushed for the creation of residential "She-She-She" camps. Washington lent her plea an indifferent ear, but Mrs. Roosevelt was not an easily-deterred woman. Unwavering in her focus, she campaigned aggressively until she saw the realization of her project. Camp Tera was the first established. By 1936, there were ninety camps established. The She-She-She camps never got the financial and political support of the Cs. Nationwide, only 8,500 women benefited from this program.[1]

courtesy of the FDR Presidential Library

The department of labor was assigned the task of administering the enrollment of youth in the program. Enrollees were referred through their State Selection agent to the War Department, which gave them the necessary medical examinations. The Army was also assigned to the construction, operation, and maintenance of the work camps.

The Departments of Agriculture and Interior were charged with the direction and coordination of work projects on state and private lands.

The U.S. Forest Service, a division of the Agricultural department, performed work on National Forests. The National Park Service executed work on National Parks and Monuments.

Nationally, 24,000 Local Experienced Men (LEM) and 24,000 WWI veterans were hired at $45 a month to serve as project leaders for CCC camps and to supervise the crews. They were older men, between the age of twenty-five and forty, recruited from nearby communities, generally unemployed, and with expertise in carpentry, masonry, logging, dynamite, and mechanics.

In his radio fireside chat of July 17, 1933, President Roosevelt addressed the CCC recruits with these words:

[1] **Eleanor Roosevelt: Volume II, 1933-1938,** by Cook, Blanche Wiesen, Viking Press, NY 1999, 88-91.

FDR's programs were often referred to as the "Alphabet Soup" (CCC, WPA, etc). He responded to critics by saying, "It's neither fish nor fowl. But whatever it is, it will taste good to the people."

"Men of the Civilian Conservation Corps, I think of you as a visible token of encouragement to the whole country. You—nearly 300,000 strong—are evidence that the nation is still strong enough and broad enough to look after its citizens.

"You are evidence that we are seeking to get away as fast as we possibly can from soup kitchens and free rations, because the government is paying you wages and maintaining you for actual work—work which is needed now and for the future and which will bring a definite financial return to the people of the nation.

"Through you the nation will graduate a fine group of strong young men, clean-living, trained to self-discipline and, above all, willing and proud to work for the joy of working."

courtesy of Douglas Key Renny

Barracks #4677 Co. CCC Irons, MI. Paul 'Charles Atlas' Oberg is in the background. Right, Douglas Key Renny, Left, Harold 'Deadeye' Mason.

"We're civilians living under military rules. We're fed, housed and clothed, not a bad deal. Our bellies are full and our money is going home to feed our parents and siblings."

Signing on the Dotted Line

"We were more or less destitute and, at six-teen, I was the oldest child of a black family in Detroit. I enrolled in the Cs to send money to Mom." —Reverend William Elum

Although the initial applicant's age had been set between eighteen and twenty-five, by 1937, it was changed to accept into the Corps any young man, otherwise qualified, if "unemployed and in need of employment." Reverend Elum, cited above, benefited from these new rules.

Edward Hartzell tried to stretch the limits a bit further. It worked—for a while. "I went into the Cs office and boldly lied about my age. I was only fifteen and a half and was released when my fib was discovered. Unlike my two friends who quit because tree planting was 'too back breaking,' I would have loved to stay."

As one can tell from the following testimonials, the majority of applicants enrolled to escape abject poverty and to offer a better life for their dependents.

"My dad lost his job and the house mortgage. We needed money to survive. I was seventeen years old and volunteered in the Cs to help out my family." Marvin Bond

"I had no education and was too small for many jobs. I applied at the local welfare center." John Gilmour

"I would have worked on a farm where they provided you with $1 a day and only two meals. The Cs gave you three. So I joined."

—Elmer Leach

Farin N. Hilton, 1st Lt. Inf. Res. Commandi

Newaygo Camp

"My dad had been laid off from Bud Wheel and went into the Cs after some friends told him about it. He always said that, as a black man with white leaders, it required a lot of adjustments." Rainelle Burton, daughter of Bonner Burton, CCC veteran

"My two older brothers had gone into the Cs to support our family. It was my turn." Charles Crafard

"I was a shy, rural boy with seven siblings. I think my dad signed me up." Robert Elmer Dodge

"There was no work. A fellow Ottawa from our community came to recruit. I liked what the Cs were doing, planting trees where there was devastation, and fighting erosion." George Yannett, Grand Traverse Band, of Chippewa and Ottawa Indians

"There were nine of us kids. Dad needed money." Gerald McNeil

Leo Lamar Athey heard about the Cs from friends and relatives and upped and went. "I lived in a small town and went to work at a very young age. The CCC program was common knowledge, and I knew two guys who had gone before me in a camp near Roger City. Since I was an outdoorsy youth it was a good fit."

Camp Superintendent

"FDR's program was quite well-known to alleviate young men's suffering. The CCC was much better than working for a potato farm, earning $15 a month, plus food and lodging. The outdoors attracted me and I wanted some experience using tools and axes. The Sheriff of Kent County sponsored me." Frank Munger

"A friend of the family was going to camp, so I went too." Arthur Barnes

"My parents had died and I was raised by my uncle and aunt whom I called Mom and Pa. I was of a curious temperament and spent a lot of time exploring outdoors. My best friend signed up and I was not going to let him go without me." Ray Larson

Don Ashcroft was getting in trouble; the Cs gave him an opportunity to turn a new leaf. "I was an out-of-work, troubled youth. Not a good combination. My welfare agent told me about the CCC and I thought it would be a different experience."

Michael Rataj was "heading for the juvenile detention center. That day, I grabbed a pair of shoes

> "Money sent home paid for my sister's education. She became a teacher."
>
> —John Selesky

OATH OF ENROLLMENT

(Upon entering the CCC, each enrollee subscribed to the following oath. It is a contract between the enrollee and the U.S. Government, and should be lived up to in each respect.)

I, _____ , do solemnly swear that the information given above as to my status is correct. I agree to remain in the Civilian Conservation Corps for the period terminating at the discretion of the United States between _____ unless sooner released by proper authority, and that I will obey those in authority and observe all the rules and regulations thereof to the best of my ability and will accept such allowances as may be provided pursuant to law and regulations promulgated pursuant thereto. I understand and agree that any injury received or disease contracted by me while a member of the Civilian Conservation Corps cannot be made the basis of any claim against the government, except such as I may be entitled to under the act of September 7, 1916, and that I shall not be entitled to any allowances upon release from camp, except transportation in kind to the place at which I was accepted for enrollment. I understand further that any articles issued to me by the United States Government for use while a member of the Civilian Conservation Corps are, and remain, property of the United States Government and that willful destruction, loss, sale or disposal of such property renders me financially responsible for the cost thereof and liable to trial in the civil courts. I understand further that any infraction of the rules or regulations of the Civilian Conservation Corps renders me liable to expulsion therefrom. So help me God.

From: "Your CCC Handbook For Enrollees" Happy Days Publishing Co., Inc., Washington, D.C.

courtesy of Frank Munger

"Mom had passed away the year before. I was too small to get a job in a factory. In my town of Ionia, it was said that 'after school graduation you went to the Ionia prison or worked for it.' I had better dreams for myself and my family."

—Waldo "Red" Fisher

from a store outdoor display and ran away, straight into our local beat cop, Tony, who was hiding behind a pole to smoke a cigarette. In those times, cops were not allowed to smoke while on duty. He nabbed me and dragged me home to give me a walloping. With so many fathers absent, looking for jobs, cops were our father figures. Fathers did not waste time with words, you were often belted. When Tony was done, my mother said, 'now give him one for me.' Which he did, and signed me up for the Cs at the police station. I did not disappoint him and put my life back on track."

Clark Curry had heard that the Cs provided good training. "I had not finished high school and wanted to further my education. My boss said he'd keep my job for me when I returned from the Cs. He did and I got a promotion as soon as I got back. A funny thing: a white CCC guy who was to become my best friend had never seen a black guy before me."

William Tylutki pursued dreams too. "I was a street kid from Dearborn, but my high school teacher kept telling me that 'there was a better life for me out there.' And there was—The CCC."

Walter Wildey was chomping at the bit. "I grew up with an axe! Couldn't wait to use it in the Cs."

Douglas Key Renny, a mild-mannered young fellow from Detroit, had two brothers-in-law in the Cs. He was seeking adventure, something different to do. He got both.

Wayne Hamilton explained with a twinkle in his eyes that "I was—still am—built close to the ground and was meant to work close to it! I was too short for other jobs. Planting red and white pine trees was ideal for my height."

For John Selesky the Cs was a natural fit. "As a youth I was involved in the Nancy Brown refor-estation project where school kids donated pen-nies for planting trees."[1]

[1] Annie Louise Brown, a.k.a. Nancy Brown, was a *Detroit News* columnist. In 1929, she raised money from her readers for the reforestation of 560 acres in Michigan.

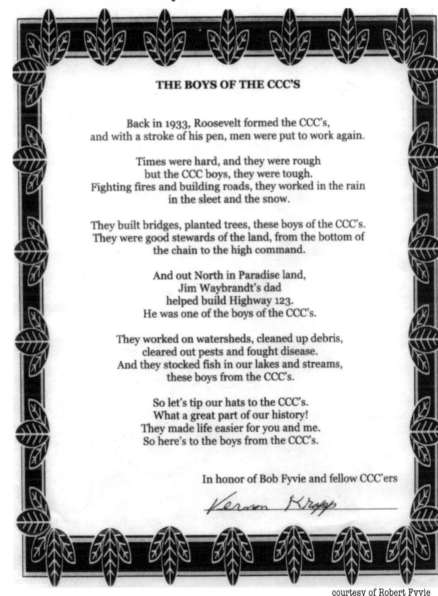

THE BOYS OF THE CCC'S

Back in 1933, Roosevelt formed the CCC's,
and with a stroke of his pen, men were put to work again.

Times were hard, and they were rough
but the CCC boys, they were tough.
Fighting fires and building roads, they worked in the rain
in the sleet and the snow.

They built bridges, planted trees, these boys of the CCC's.
They were good stewards of the land, from the bottom of
the chain to the high command.

And out North in Paradise land,
Jim Waybrandt's dad
helped build Highway 123.
He was one of the boys of the CCC's.

They worked on watersheds, cleaned up debris,
cleared out pests and fought disease.
And they stocked fish in our lakes and streams,
these boys from the CCC's.

So let's tip our hats to the CCC's.
What a great part of our history!
They made life easier for you and me.
So here's to the boys from the CCC's.

In honor of Bob Fyvie and fellow CCC'ers

Vernon Krupp

courtesy of Robert Fyvie

Retreat

"My father, James Chester Underhill, had never lived in a rural setting and was quite apprehensive." Diana Dinverno

Courtesy Newaygo County Society of History and Genealogy

THE CCC PRAYER

First week in Camp:

"Now I lay me down to sleep,
    I pray the Lord my soul to keep.
Grant no other C.C. take
    My shoes and socks before I wake.
Lord, keep me while I snore,
    And keep my bed upon the floor."

Months later:

"Our father, who art in Washington,
    Please, dear father, let me stay,
    Do not drive me now away.
Wipe away my scalding tears,
    And let me stay a couple of years."
                —Robert "Rosy" Pullen,
                    Written in April 1937

courtesy of Douglas Key Renny

Enrollee singing "saddle your blues to a wild mustang." Looking down on Little Manistee River. The bulge in his coat is his lunch, trying to keep his sandwiches from freezing.

A Bunch of Scared Kids

"I was an Eagle Scout and was afraid that guys would think me a 'sissy' if they found out." —Gerard Perry

"This is to certify that your son has been accepted for enrollment in the Civilian Conservation Corps and has been transferred to Company No..." This is how William Tylutki's parents learned of their son's enrollment in the Cs for six months, with the option to re-enlist in six-month increments for up to two years. He had not told them of his application.

Families received the news with excitement and gratitude for sons and brothers willing to improve themselves and provide financial survival for their loved ones. Twenty-five of the thirty dollars earned by the enrollees were to be sent to dependents every month. In exchange, these young males would work a forty-hour week in jobs related to conservation. Camps were run by the Army, and enrollees, although civilian, would have to comply with its rules.

Some families gave their young men a last word of wisdom before saying goodbye.

Robert Fyvie's dad told him that "the way to win a fight is to stay out of it."

Reverend William Elum's father, a preacher, had taught him that "you choose to turn a situation into a positive or negative thing. You can learn from both. It's up to you."

They made it! Having passed physical examination and vaccinations, they were official CCC enrollees. Now what?

> "I was away from my family for the first time and it was awfully hard. I was lonesome."
> —Leo Lamar Athey

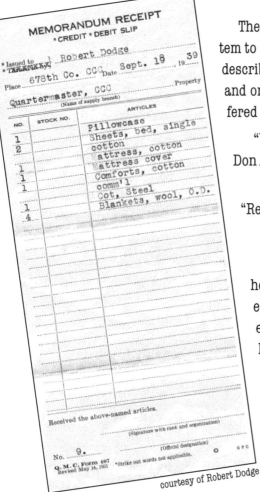

MEMORANDUM RECEIPT
* CREDIT * DEBIT SLIP

Issued to .... Robert Dodge
678th Co. CCC Date Sept. 18 , 19 39
Place ....
Quartermaster, CCC .... Property
(Name of supply branch)

NO.	STOCK NO.	ARTICLES
1		Pillowcase
2		Sheets, bed, single cotton
1		Mattress, cotton
1		Mattress cover
1		Comforts, cotton comm'l
1		Cot, Steel
4		Blankets, wool, O.D.

Received the above-named articles.

(Signature with rank and organization)

No. 9.
(Official designation)
Q.M.C. Form 487   * Strike out words not applicable.
Revised May 14, 1931

courtesy of Robert Dodge

The Army had requisitioned the nation's transportation system to move the new enrollees to training camps for what many described as "a life-changing experience." Packed in Army trucks and on their way to induction centers, many of the "boys" suffered some form of trepidation.

"We were a bunch of scared kids and tried not to show it." Don Ashcroft

"All of us were homesick. It was difficult at first." Waldo "Red" Fisher

"I used to stutter and was nervous." Gerald McNeil

Reverend William Elum was less nervous than most; he'd been raised strictly by his father, who was a preacher. He expected to adjust easily to Army discipline. A few enrollees went in with friends or relatives and were not lonely. Ray Larson had his best friend and Elmer Leach had his brother and cousin. Brothers were not supposed to be in the Cs at the same time, but a few tricky fellows managed to sneak their way in.

And, of course, in each group there is one self-assured young man, Frank Munger, who thought that "I was a man of the world and was not frightened. I had been separated from my family in summers when I worked for farmers and felt at home wherever I was. In some ways I was well prepared for the strong values and discipline of the CCC. I had learned to work very hard for farmers."

For some administrative reason, Michael Rataj could not be sent to camp immediately. The Cs put him up at the local YMCA for three weeks, "a crime prevention approach."

Ready to go, Harrison, May 1, 1935

courtesy of Douglas Key Renny

Camp Custer, Trout Lake, Walhalla; the locations might be different but the training was identical. First, they were indoctrinated, explained the rules and code of behavior—mostly Army regulations—and took the CCC oath. Next they trooped to Supply to collect their allotment. (See list from R. Dodge's receipt). Most of it came from WWI surplus, especially clothes. The clothing package included: shoes, socks, undershirt and underwear, 100% wool pants, a belt and flannel shirts, a necktie, dress cap and a WWI uniform for dress purposes. Frank Munger still remembers how scratchy and hot they were. Some work clothing was also provided: overalls, working gloves and hat.

Cartoons from a CCC scrapbook depict the ill-fitting clothes of recruits.

HOW EACH ENROLLEE WOULD LIKE TO DRESS—

GOLLY

HOW FIRST ISSUE OF UNIFORMS FIT!

courtesy of Annick Hivert-Carthew

Attire and gear came in all sizes and were distributed regardless of the weight and height of their recipients. "Clothes came in two sizes: too big and too small. It was a free-for-all. You grabbed your lot and traded with others." Michael Rataj

Each man was told he was responsible for the cleanliness of his attire. Some decided to hire a local washer woman to launder and press their clothes.

Enrollees also received toilet and mess kits with a towel and a canteen, a steel cot with a cotton mattress and bedding, and a metal disk with each individual's number inscribed on it. Anything else—cigarettes, candy bars, toothpaste—they'd have to purchase themselves at the Camp canteen store.

They were assigned to sleeping quarters. In the barracks, bunks were lined up against the walls. A demonstration and practice of making beds Army style—so tight you could "bounce a nickel on the blanket"—took place.

Trucks to take enrollees to camps.

courtesy of Douglas Key Renny

Days were lived military style

6:00 A.M. Reveille

Calisthenics

Breakfast

Roll call and inspection

7:45 A.M. departure by trucks for workplace

One hour for lunch served in the field (whenever delivery trucks got there)

4:00 P.M. return to camp followed by private time for recreation

5:30 P.M. dinner

Free time or classes.

10 P.M. lights out

Enrollees could leave camp to seek entertainment in the nearby community, but had to be back by bedtime.

courtesy of Leo Lamar Athey

Leo Lamar Athey, Isle Royale, crew unloading. 4:00 P.M.

courtesy of Leo Lamar Athey

Isle Royale, Leo Lamar Athey sitting in boat.

Day trucks at Marion, Camp Harrison.

courtesy of Douglas Key Renny

First Impressions

"The land is barren; what the hell am I doing here?" —Gerard Perry

On 2 May 1933, Detroit and Hamtramck boys, fresh from training Camp Custer, and the first Michigan enrollees to work in the Upper Peninsula, were shipped to a remote location in the Hiawatha National Forest. Stunned, disoriented, and tired by a trip by train, ferry, and truck, they had to grab axes and tools to chop trees and clean up brush to set up camp.

Most camps began at virgin sites and involved intense physical labor and a certain amount of toughness—sleeping in rain and snow inside pyramid or bell tents and eating meals outdoors until tarpaper barracks could be erected. "I'm six-foot tall and had snow up to my armpits!" commented Philipps. One enrollee's shoes froze overnight, not a happy discovery.

courtesy of Douglas Key Renny

Many of the Cs had never been in a rural area before enrolling.

"The only possessions most of us had were the clothes on our backs. On the way to Camp Steuben, a few guys in my truck struggled with English and others chatted together in their native tongues. All of us marveled at the beauty of the Upper Peninsula scenery."

—Don Ashcroft

Mud Lake, Irons. Looking at the wilderness.

courtesy of Douglas Key Renny

Eventually camps would develop into proper and well-run little villages with kitchen and mess hall, library, educational and school buildings, latrines and bathhouses, infirmary, and places for entertainment and relaxation. The boys slept in tarpaper barracks with a simple wooden floor on the inside. Officers had their own private quarters.

"We got off the trucks at the site of future Camp Garth, Company 671, in an area of desolation. There was nothing there. CCC officers and a navy doctor had come with us. We cleared the land, erected tents for bathhouse, galleys, and first aid shack. Tents were set up in rectangular shapes, far enough from latrines and galleys. There were about ten boys sleeping on cots inside the tent. We'd arrived just in time for blueberry season and devoured pounds of them. One fellow missed home so much, he couldn't stop crying. He was released and sent back home." Frank Munger

"I saw my first seagulls when we arrived on Isle Royale in May. To look out on the water and not see the other shore was impressive. That's a lot of water! It was still cold and icy and we were to sleep on cots in tents with wooden floors." Leo Lamar Athey

"On our way to Houghton Lake, it began to sleet." Clark Curry

"After three weeks in transit at Camp Trout, I was put on a train, then a boat across the Straits with the train on it. Train and recruits got off the boat and continued the journey across the Upper Peninsula, stopping along the way to pick up more recruits, all of them pretty unsure and nervous. After dropping us in the middle of nowhere, a truck arrived to take us to Camp Mackinac, twenty-six miles from Newberry. In my head, I fully expected to spend the next six months behind bars or barbed wires, but there was nothing there!" Michael Rataj

"I did not know then that I was about to experience the best years of my life. I had grown up with an axe and couldn't wait to use it." Walter Wildey

At Camp Steuben in the winter of 1934-35, Don Ashcroft, on a survey crew, had to "crawl on our hands and knees through the branches of evergreen trees, dragging our equipment behind us through deep snow."

"Camp Marquette was reserved for Native Americans and we came from all over." George Yannett, Odawa, Grand Traverse Band of Chippewa and Ottawa Indians

Camp Norrie, 1939.

"We were not allowed to build a fire until we'd started working. I realized then that I was not home." Johnnie Johnston, "Camp Forgotten," documentary by William Jamerson

According to Waldo "Red" Fisher, "kids who were headed for trouble learned right away that there was no room for it in the Cs."

"I had never seen so much snow as at Camp Evelyn. It was a shock!" Marvin Bond

courtesy of Leo Lamar Athey

Beaver Dam, Isle Royale.

courtesy of Douglas Key Renny

Douglas Key
Renny driving safely.

courtesy of Douglas Key Renny

Douglas Key Renny
bringing in wood for barrack's wood
stove, winter '35-'36. Advt: Wanted, one
oil burner in good condition!

courtesy of Ray Larson

Newaygo CCC, Ray Larson sitting on his
truck.

Settling In

"We arrived pretty rebellious, but it took us two minutes to know who the boss was."
—Michael Rataj

"Home sweet home." Well, not at first. For most youth, introduction to camp life came as a shock.

"The train dropped us off in the middle of nowhere. A truck was waiting to take us to Camp Mackinac. A big guy came out and bellowed, 'My name is Mr. Morrison. Since I am a civilian and also a sergeant, you're going to call me SIR, S-I-R, not SARGE, S-A-R-G-E. If you do, you'll be looking for that word in the dictionary until hell freezes over. Only my friends call me that; and I don't have any.'

"One guy said, 'I'm going back on the train.' They chased after him and put him back in the truck." Michael Rataj

Leo Lamar Athey's first thought was, "What am I doing here?" And a few days later, "Showers were supposed to be hot, but...And we could rarely swim in Lake Superior; it was often just above freezing."

"Nobody had prepared us for this. We arrived pretty rebellious, but it took us two minutes to know who the boss was. The older boys quickly advised us, 'not

> "When I first arrived, a blue racer crossed near me and got tangled up in my laces. I fell next to the snake. I had never seen one before and was petrified."
>
> —William Tylutki

Driving to the gravel pit.

courtesy of Douglas Key Renny

Loaded trucks had the right of way; empties hit the brush.

"At Camp Garth, I was introduced to a fellow who was the spitting image of me—or I of him—same build and facial traits. We were often confused for one another. In line for food, this fellow would go up to be served. When I went up, they said, 'What are you doing here, you've already been served!' Many decades later we still look very similar."

—Frank Munger

to break the rules because if the officers did not do anything about it, they would.' Besides, we were mostly city boys and they loved to frighten us with tales of bear attacks and snake bites.

"'SIR' hollered for the first few days to make us understand who the boss was. Most of us needed strong discipline anyway. After a while we became like family and he'd talk to us like an uncle or a father would. Our attitude changed pretty rapidly. From cocky and rambunctious, we learned to show respect and to reply, 'Yes, SIR.'" Michael Rataj

"When military officers were around you stood to attention, like in the Army, but you did not salute them. We were civilians; there were no military discipline and drills." John Gilmour

As hard as it was, the CCC offered solace and refuge for a few fellows. Michael Rataj asked a young black man from Los Angeles, "What are you doing in the Cs so far from home?"

The guy replied. "I used to sell drugs and I want to live to be twenty-one."

"Camp was less crowded than Detroit and it was clean. I enjoyed that." Reverend William Elum

"Houghton Lake was racially mixed. We had no problems, but by affinity I socialized mostly with Blacks." Arthur Barnes

Pranks

"You're bound to play tricks once you put fifty boys together."
—Charles Crafard

According to Cameron Glynn, new recruits were "innocent babes thrown to the wolves."

One night Don Ashcroft went to Manistique and came back to camp at 2:00 A.M. to find his bed tied to the rafters in the ceiling. "I figured that waking forty fellows in the early hours of the morning was not a very healthy thing for me to do. Instead of untying my bunk, I pulled the blankets down and slept on the floor for the rest of the night."

Taking advantage of rookies was common practice in the CCC camps. Pranks ranged from the usual short-sheeting to dropping city boys in the woods at night after feeding them tall tales of deadly wild boar and bear attacks and venomous rattlers' bites.

"We used to put pebbles in small boxes of matches and rattle them at night to scare city boys." William Tylutki

"I left greenhorns in the woods at night to find their way back to camp." Elmer Leach

Regular and benign hazing included nailing shoes to the floor or filling them up with syrup. Recruits were sent to "borrow a left-hand monkey wrench" or some other non-existent tool.

Some companies were creative. "A new bunch of kids arrived from Chicago. We told them that the flag pole had to be watered regularly and we made them do it."

—Stan Ward

Ed Schultz playing in the snow.

courtesy of Douglas Key Renny

Another veteran informed newcomers to stay by the watch tower the whole night, and if an officer came by to ask what they were doing, to tell him to "mind his own business" because senior boys often pretended to be officers to make new recruits do silly things. You can guess what happened. A real officer discovered them. Those boys discovered the joys of KP a little sooner than most.

Some tricks were rather dangerous. "My job was to sharpen axes for the crew. I sharpened them extra sharp for the city boys. One kid sliced his shoe open. The LEM (Local Experienced Man) said he would do it from then on." Philipps

Others were a little wicked. "The older men initiated us by throwing us off the docks into the Black River with our clothes on. In turn, we threw people fully dressed in Lake Superior."[1]

[1]Ray Larson, **The Larsons,** p 43

Some boys were not so easy to trick.

"The older boys tried to play tricks on me, but I was too quick! Later, I sent new recruits on Snipe hunts and told them not to come back until they'd caught one." Gerald McNeil.

"When I first got to camp, they said that everyone had to be dunked in the rain barrel. I grabbed hold of a big guy and said, 'Sure, and he's coming with me.' After that they left me alone." Robert Elmer Dodge

Basically, older boys "loved picking on younger guys!" Waldo "Red" Fisher

courtesy of Douglas Key Renny

Douglas Key Renny having fun. Barrack 4, 677 Cop. CCC Camp Irons, 1936.

Keeping a sense of humor.

courtesy of Frank Munger

NORTH HIGGINS LK STATE PARK WISH YOU

SEASONS GREETINGS

CHECK ONE OF THE FOLLOWING MALES IN EACH GROUP THAT YOU THINK SHOULD
BEAR THE TITLE ABOVE THEIR NAME ****

NEATEST ENROLLEE

___ Ray Lysewski
___ Ernest Turton
___ Ollie Jankoviak

BEST WORKER

___ George Donald
___ Tom Stevens
___ Ollie Jankoviak

MOST POPULAR ENROLLEE

___ Tom Stevens
___ Pat LaRoue
___ Steve Szyllagyi

MOST COURTEOUS

___ Ollie Jankoviak
___ Tom Pekich
___ Glen Osborne

BIGGEST SHIEK

___ Paul Thibadeau
___ Stanley Rowell
___ John Ivanski

CHAMP GOLDBRICKER

___ Merle Flanery
___ William Horvath
___ Joseph Prouo

CAMP CHOW HOUND

___ Hobart Striker
___ Theodore Goodyear
___ Tom Pekich

BIGGEST GROUCH

___ Leonard Dietz
___ Hobart Striker
___ Herman Stremler

BEST ATHLETE

___ Verne VanDenberg
___ Carl Cox
___ Hamry Asenouts

BIGGEST CHISZLER

___ Edward Tyvela
___ Leonard Dietz
___ Phil Eeingenburg

courtesy of Robert Dodge

Voting sheet from Camp Walhalla.

Douglas Key Renny up a tree.
"Can you see me?"

courtesy of Douglas Key Renny

33 • PRANKS

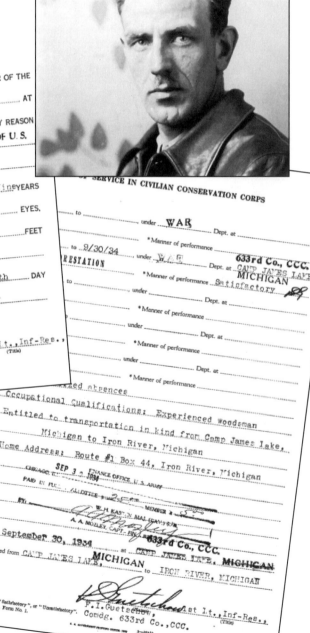

Certificate of Discharge
from
Civilian Conservation Corps

TO ALL WHOM IT MAY CONCERN:

THIS IS TO CERTIFY THAT * Albert Collins CC6-E4617 A MEMBER OF THE

CIVILIAN CONSERVATION CORPS, WHO WAS ENROLLED May 22nd, 1934 AT
                                                    (Date)

CAMP JAMES LAKE, MICHIGAN HONORABLY IS HEREBY DISCHARGED THEREFROM, BY REASON

OF ** EXPIRATION OF TERM OF ENROLLMENT FOR CONVENIENCE OF U.S.

SAID Albert Collins WAS BORN IN Belfast

IN THE STATE OF Ireland WHEN ENROLLED HE WAS Twenty-Nine YEARS

OF AGE AND BY OCCUPATION A Painter HE HAD Blue EYES,

Brown HAIR, Ruddy COMPLEXION, AND WAS Five FEET

Eleven INCHES IN HEIGHT. HIS COLOR WAS WHITE

GIVEN UNDER MY HAND AT CAMP JAMES LAKE, MICHIGAN THIS Thirtieth DAY

OF September ONE THOUSAND NINE HUNDRED AND Thirty-Four

F.I.Guetschow, 1st Lt., Inf-Res.,
Comdg. 633rd Co., CCC, (Title)

C.C.C. Form No. 2
April 6, 1933

* Insert name, as "John J. Doe".
** Give reason for discharge.

—— SERVICE IN CIVILIAN CONSERVATION CORPS

... to ... under WAR Dept. at ...
* Manner of performance
... to 9/30/34 under WAR 633rd Co., CCC,
RESTATION Dept. at CAMP JAMES LAKE
MICHIGAN
... to ... under ... Dept. at ... * Manner of performance Satisfactory
* Manner of performance
... to ... under ... Dept. at ...
* Manner of performance
... under ... Dept. at ...
* Manner of performance

...ized absences

Occupational Qualifications: Experienced Woodsman

Entitled to transportation in kind from Camp James Lake,
Michigan to Iron River, Michigan

Home Address: Route #1 Box 44, Iron River, Michigan

SEP 3 0 1934 FINANCE OFFICE, U.S. ARMY
PAID IN FULL ALLOTTEE $25.00 MEMBER $ .5

W.H. KASTEN MAJ (CAVE)R
A.A. MOZLEY, CAPT. INF., 633rd Co., CCC,
MICHIGAN

HONORABLY
Discharged: September 30, 1934 at CAMP JAMES LAKE, MICHIGAN

Transportation furnished from CAMP JAMES LAKE, to IRON RIVER, MICHIGAN

F.I.Guetschow, 1st Lt., Inf-Res.,
Comdg. 633rd Co., CCC. (Title)

* Use words "Excellent", "Satisfactory", or "Unsatisfactory".
** To be taken from C.C.C. Form No. 1.

Albert Collins, shown here with his
CCC Certificate, is the brother-in-law of
Douglas Key Renny. Albert Collins was
a LEM for three to four years at Gibbs
City Camp, near Iron River, planting
trees. He'd come to the U.S. from his
native Ireland when he was nineteen.
He was the father of two and lived
nearby when he applied for the job.

courtesy of Henry Renny

LEMs (Local Experienced Men)

"LEMs were looked up to. We respected their experience and willingness to pass along their skills with tools and dynamite."
—Frank Munger

Pretty green and untrained in CCC skills—carpentry, masonry, logging, dynamite, and mechanics—young recruits needed to be taught the use and safety of tools to execute planned reforestation. Local Experienced Men (LEM) and WWI veterans were hired at $45 a month for that purpose. They were older men, between the ages of twenty-five and forty, recruited from nearby communities, generally unemployed, and with the appropriate expertise to serve as project leaders to supervise the crews. Many interviewees stated that relationships with LEMs and WWI veterans were much like fathers and sons.

Military men, a commanding officer, a junior officer, and a medical officer headed camps of civilians. Camps were run with Army-like rules, but no military drills and punishments occurred. Returning AWOLs were simply fined and given suitable punishments such as KP duty. At the end of a working day, sergeants would climb in the young men's trucks to compliment them on a well-done job. Michael Rataj

"I think of it like a boxer; you know how he gets one minute rest? Well, this was our rest—away from all the boxing, the getting beat down. We were fed, we had hard work, and we had medicine."

—Michael Rataj

> "I saw what hard times really were. When we are all gone, no one will understand what hard times really are. There is a big difference between then and now."
> —Waldo "Red" Fisher

Bill O'Brien, a favorite LEM of Douglas Key Renny

courtesy of Douglas Key Renny

recalls Mr. Morrison, a sergeant, telling him, "Mike, you made some mistakes but you will not make them again." Mr. Morrison was strict but fair. "There was no rancor. Once you'd been punished, both parties forgot about it and you were not passed over for promotion. Mr. Morrison became a friend, but not a buddy.

"Our superintendent of work details was going to be laid off by the Police Department. The CCC employed him to teach and supervise woodworking. The LEMs were mostly out-of-work men who were willing to 'recycle' their skills to obtain some money for their families. One day I discovered that leaders bent rules when compassion was needed. My teammates and I were checking the fish we had previously planted and discovered that some tagged fish were caught in traps. All our fish were tagged with i.d. and no poaching was allowed. 'What shall we do?' we asked him. 'Let them be. People are feeding their families.' "

Douglas Key Renny, a young immigrant from Scotland, "made good friends with LEMs." He kept in touch after an honorable discharge from the Cs, especially with Bill O'Brien, whom he often visited.

Reverend William Elum stated that "Leaders were fair, no problems in camp, only in the nearby community. The first time I went to town I was arrested, most likely because I was black. After that I stayed at the camp."

But Bonner Burton, another African American, did not share these feelings about the Cs. He used to complain to his daughter that "enrollees were black and leaders white," and that as a black man he did not "get many breaks." He labored hard under very tough conditions; "factory work did not seem so hard after that."

"At Camp Marquette, a Native American camp, we had white and Native American leaders. I was too young to be a leader, but I'd loved to have been one. The CCC treated me very well, better than the Army in WWII." George Yannett, Odawa, Grand Traverse Band of Chippewa and Ottawa Indians

Enrollees who had specific skills and demonstrated some leadership qualities had the chance to become LEMs and leaders. Many seized this opportunity to show their mettle.

Reverend William Elum earned stripes through his diligence. He was picked to be barrack leader, supervising its cleanliness and order, and was promoted to the fire tower watch. He also learned to be a surveyor.

Camp Newaygo officers. courtesy of Newaygo County Society of History and Genealogy

Cameron Glynn joined the Cs at twenty-four, after being a sergeant in the National Guard. He was employed as company mechanic as well as the leader responsible for morning calisthenics and camp order. He liked the Cs so much that he managed to stretch his stay by two extra months over the limit.

Gerard Perry got a surveyor job because he had been an Eagle Scout. He started as leader of a crew of sixteen men and, later, eight crews of sixteen men each. One day, the first sergeant called him in the Captain's office and said, "I need a first sergeant and I think I've found him."

Perry looked around. There was no one but him. "Who, me?"

As he accepted the job, he warned the Captain that, "he was to run the camp his way."

"Fine," replied the Captain, "so long as it is the Army way."

As for LEMs and leaders employed to train the "boys," Albert Collins was a young Irishman who worked as a LEM for several years at Gibbs City Camp, near Iron River. He expressed well the shared thoughts of these "father" figures. Collins often told his family that he enjoyed passing skills along to juniors. "They were eager to learn, the teaching was fun, and my charges viewed me more as a pal than a leader. Both parties enjoyed a pleasant atmosphere of camaraderie."

Besides, being a leader offered a huge financial reward. "After four months in the Cs, I became a leader with a pay of $45 a month. The extra $15 did not go home. I like that!" Bernard McGill

105⁰ F in the shade, July 1936.

Fire calls, going east towards Irons.

Digging by hand a gravel pit
for fire trail improvement.

Enrollees taking a
break from digging trenches.

CCC heavy
equipment clearing
land.

Forest Fires

"Your feet are always burning; your throat is on fire from smoke; you stink like a pig and your hands are hot."

—Michael Rataj

For decades, Michigan forests had suffered from devastating wildfires. Before Roosevelt's Tree Army, sometimes called the "College of Calluses," could reclaim the Michigan landscape and begin reforestation, these fires had to be eliminated and prevented.

"Some of the fellows were called out to fight fires." Frank Munger's diary, May 6, 1934.

For the first years of the program, Michigan CCC (MCCC) enrollees spent much of their time fighting fires and building fire trail breaks to shield Michigan's enormous forest resources from further destruction. Equipment was rudimentary: portable eight-pound pumps where lake or river water was accessible, and simple shovels. Each man had his own shovel, engraved with his name because "it fitted your hand exactly the way you wanted it." According to Edward Hartzell, in a fire outside of Kalkaska, "little hand sprayers were useful only if you could keep them filled."

George Yannett, an Odawa from the Grand Traverse Band of Chippewa and Ottawa Indians, ruefully confessed that, "I never thought I could get hurt. There I was with a spade and a hoe, in the middle of a blaze!"

courtesy of Douglas Key Renny

Rushing to the site of a fire.

[1] Adapted from "Roosevelt's Tree Army, Michigan Civilian Conservation Corps," by Roger L. Rosentreter

"We had leather gloves. Our hands were hot, and we were tired."

—Clarence Springer

The CCC program had been put together so rapidly that industry got caught short of supplies of hoes, shovels, and axes. Michigan State University's forestry department and the University of Michigan came to the rescue and lent the Cs tools.

In only two years, the MCCC established:

3,000 miles of truck trails to provide access to fires

8 lookout towers

275 miles of firebreaks

Cleared 40,000 acres of land to reduce fire hazard

Spent 54,000 man days fighting fires[1]

Enrollees worked in long and exhausting twelve-hour shifts. The day shift usually began at 3:30 A.M. and continued until the arrival of the night shift at 6:00 P.M. Night crews toiled by lantern light. Many had never seen fires of such proportions and were scared. One day Stan Ward was hemmed in by fire and still remembers his fear. "I thought I would die."

Sometimes fire was located in a difficult place to reach by trucks and the transport of food and supplies became unreliable and the crews experienced shortages. Perishables would arrive spoilt and were eaten anyway. That, as well as poor sanitary conditions, provoked unpleasant outbursts of dysentery.

When Isle Royale, home to CCC camps, caught on fire, it took 1800 men three months to put it out, working in shifts twenty hours a day. In spite of this, 20% of the island burned. Fire devastated 31,000 acres of Presque Isle State Forest and 36,000 acres of the Ottawa National Forest.

Fighting fires was tough. It required guts and stamina. Frank Munger fought a huge forest fire night and day for six weeks in a row in the small town of Perkins. Munger's company was stationed at Camp Garth and "rode sixty miles in trucks each way. We were exhausted."

One tough veteran, William Tylutki, recalls that he got "no new blisters." His hands were already "quite worn by raising crops at home."

These ordeals wrought a fair share of human tragedies and heroism. In William Jamerson's documentary, "Camp Forgotten," a veteran speaks of one Andrew D. Lindgren, a leader who, trapped by a blaze in the Huron National Forest, led his guys out of danger and, thinking that two recruits were still hemmed in by fire, went back in. Mr. Lindgren perished fifty yards from safety. The two recruits had escaped earlier. Mr. Lindgren posthumously received the North American Forest Fire Medal of bravery.[2]

The second phase of fire control involved the construction of lookout towers for early fire detection, with connecting phone lines between towers and camps.

William Tylutki, always looking for ways of going home, worked in such a tower for extra days of vacation. One day he noticed a fire and was able to call camp to give its location. "It was in July and we had a hard time containing it. Once I stayed awake thirty-six hours in a row."

[2] "Roosevelt's Tree Army, Michigan Civilian Conservation Corps," by Roger Rosentreter

courtesy of Douglas Key Renny

Burning brush, January 14, 1936. Douglas Key Renny, "don't make me laugh, I have chapped lips."

Forest Service Fire wooden fire tower, between Peacock and Irons, 1936.

courtesy of Douglas Key Renny

Chittenden Tree nursery.

"I liked what we were doing; planting and fighting erosion. Each man had his own spade, because your hands got used to one. Guys carved their initials on the handle. We guarded them jealously. They were made of cast iron and steel, very heavy to work with. When we first started, everyone had blisters, then calluses."

—George Yannett, Odawa, Grand Traverse Band of Chippewa and Ottawa Indians

Pine seedlings at the Chittenden Tree nursery. The spade or "planting bar," a cast iron and steel tool, was so heavy that men now in their eighties, such as Arthur Barnes, still remember its weight. They walked miles every day, carrying a planting bar and box of seedlings.

Sod was removed from a selected area about one foot square with a "scalper." Trees were planted two feet apart, alternating Norway Pines and Jack Pines.

Reforestation

"I was built close to the ground and was meant to work close to it! Planting red and white pines was ideal for my height."
—Wayne Hamilton

Once fires were more or less under control, reforestation, lumbering, and building could begin. From 1933 to 1942, CCC "boys" not only salvaged but revitalized Michigan's landscape and park systems with their own sweat and guts. Reforestation required the establishment of nurseries. By 1936, one million seedlings were ready for planting. Later, Chittenden nursery harvested 20 million seedlings a year with the most advanced technology of the day.

Planters had to follow a strict sequence of steps and execute them quickly. It was a repetitive and backbreaking job. To motivate their charges, leaders organized competitions between crews, tents or barracks for the most planted seedlings of the day. The winning teams competed against other camps. On average, a team of men planted 20,000 seedlings a day!

courtesy of Douglas Key Renny

Three-man crew: raker, dibbler, and planter.

[1] **The Larsons**, by Ray Larson, page 43

Sometimes a tractor was sent to plow furrows for the boys to plant the seedlings in. Elmer Leach was rather proud to drive an old tractor with a double plow.

First, the planter drove the planting bar into the ground and rocked it back and forth to open a slot in the ground, one inch wide, two inches across, four to five inches deep. The seedlings were inserted into the slot. Soil was first tightened around them with the handling bar, then with the enrollees' boot heel.

At the beginning and end of each working day, enrollees loaded waiting trucks with a Number 2 shovel. Drivers were exempt from shoveling. No wonder "boys fought for that position!"

Tree planting was "easy" for some. John Gilmour joined the Cs because he was too small for other jobs. Tree planting was ideal for him.

Robert Elmer Dodge did a bit of showing off. He worked on a plowing crew. One day they drove by the school his brother attended. They stopped to show them the tractors.

Meanwhile "lumberjacks," such as Ray Larson, cleared the planting areas, taking trees down with axes freshly sharpened every morning. Nothing was wasted. Fallen or cut trees were transported to the nearest sawmill to be used as timber in the construction of state projects. "Proper lumberjacks taught us to take down large pine trees, trim them with double-bit axes, and saw them up with two-man cross-cut saws."[1]

But not everyone agreed with the decisions of the Park Service. Philipps rather proudly tells the story of the time when, "We had cleared up an area outside of camp where a huge white pine stood. The Park Service wanted to cut it down to run some lines across the area. We rushed over and convinced them to save it. That pine tree is still there now."

Job Assignments

"They asked me if I liked water and could swim. 'Yes,' I replied, dreaming of being a lifeguard. 'Good, you can wash dishes.'"
—Michael Rataj

Fire fighting and reforestation were not the only jobs available. A whole slew of posts needed to be filled and some jobs came to recruits through personal skills.

"My father, Chester Underhill, was mechanically minded, could fix anything. Father and garage grease were very much intertwined. He was a mechanic in the Cs." Diana Dinverno

"I was a farm boy and was used to handling heavy-duty equipment. A big Swede, 'Thorne,' taught me to drive bulldozers and tractors." Robert Fyvie

Throughout his youth, Stan Ward always wanted to know how trucks worked and how to fix them. At camp he volunteered to get an old Caterpillar working. After much testing, he found out that the magneto needed overhaul. He fixed it up and found the engine was running very well—backwards! He refitted the magneto the right way and it ran great. He

"I got a job through a leader. The man was repairing a truck with C boys gathered around him. He asked for a flex handle. I was the only one who knew what it was and passed it on to him. I got to drive trucks and tractors and liked doing it, as any boy would."

—Elmer Leach

Accident at the railroad track in Irons. A CCC truck was hit by a railroad snowplow.

courtesy of Douglas Key Renny

learned how to drive it and was so competent at it, he became assistant mechanic. At eighteen, he drove the truck to town with fifteen men onboard. "And you can't fool with trucks!"

One icy day, going down Mancelona Hill, Ward could not stop the truck. He narrowly missed an old eighteen-wheeler stuck across the road. The Cs had given him the confidence to go for challenges; at the bottom of the hill he told his men that they were going back to move the eighteen-wheeler. They pushed and pushed and, with the driver gunning the motor, they unstuck it.

Another time while working in the U.P., Ward heard that a two-wheel-drive snow plow had gotten stuck in three feet of snow. He drove a four-wheel-drive 1934 GMC dump truck with chains on the tires, so was sent to pull it out.

"There was this huge old tree behind the kitchen. The foreman said it had to come out. My dad worked in lumber and had trained me. I took my axe. You should have seen us chop the two-foot-wide oak. Chips were flying up! But I really wanted to be in KP. One time I went in the kitchen. Cook asked if anyone knew how to clean chickens. Fellows did not know how to pluck feathers and were throwing

"I wanted to be a cook because it was too cold outside. They first put me on KP, and then sent me to Wisconsin to cooking school. I was the only black guy there. One fellow, who was to become my best friend, had never seen a black man before. I got the highest marks in the class."

—Clark Curry

gizzards and innards. I showed them how to fry them in butter. They devoured them, and I got the job." Philipps

Other assignments came to recruits through irony.

"My first job was on the road improvement team, a grand name for picking up trash. Then I was transferred to the mess hall because I'd mentioned that I liked water and could swim! My job had some advantage; when it was cold and rainy, I was indoors, warm and dry." Michael Rataj

Special jobs required training, often carried out "on the spot." Frank Munger worked on a dynamite crew, helping to blow up stumps. "LEMs trained us to set off a charge in a rather primitive way to pull tree stumps out. Instead of electronic detonators, we used a crowbar to dig a hole to put in a stick of dynamite. When the strips of fuse lit and the flame came out, you'd better run for cover, as far as possible. The whole stump did not blow up. You hitched a team of horses hired from locals to pull out the rest of the stumps. The first time I blew a stump, I was not scared, rather excited. At eighteen, you don't fear anything. My first stump was a big event. I served on 'side' camp; twenty men assigned to advanced crew to dynamite and clear trails.

"At Camp Wyman we built a root cellar. It was big and it took us a couple of weeks to finish it. There was a lot of snow. We went to cut the pines on snowshoes. It was the first time I used them."

Arthur Barnes was trained to cut and plant trees, and to build roads. Waldo "Red" Fisher also built roads. The one leading from Newberry to Tahquamenon Falls still gives him the shivers. "It was a nightmare. Terrible black flies kept on biting us." Robert Elmer Dodge drove a Caterpillar tractor and plowed furrows to plant seedlings.

February 24, 1936, Indian Bridge, Manistee River.

courtesy of Douglas Key Renny

courtesy of Douglas Key Renny

Edward Hartzell, having sneaked in the Cs at the "old" age of fifteen, signed as a truck driver. "The officer said, 'You want wheels; we'll give you some.' They gave me a wheelbarrow and told me to work on the grease pit and septic hold out!"

> "When you went to your job, you did not do what today's youth tend to do—loaf—you got there to work."
> —Waldo "Red" Fisher

[1] **The Larsons,** by Ray Larson, page 43

Ray Larson built parking lots, restrooms, pavilions, bridges, docks and breakwaters on Lake Superior. He had a twenty-five mile ride to the work site, straight after breakfast. "It was hard work and a long day, but a beautiful place to work in. One of our most beautiful projects was a foot suspension bridge over the Black River Harbor at Lake Superior, which is still in use today. The hardest job was breaking rocks with sledge hammers for a breakwater. We had eight men cutting trees for crossbars and debarking the trunks with draw knives; a perilous job with snow on the ground."[1]

Waldo "Red" Fisher cleared streams and built fish structures. "I did that until I got arthritis in my knees so bad from the cold water. They transferred me to a fish survey crew. We checked fish caught to record growth."

Gerard Perry practiced "'scalping'—preparing the land to plant trees, 12" x 12" holes, six feet apart, with the idea that 40% would live."

Douglas Key Renny worked in the woods, cleaning streams and planting fish in Pere Marquette National Forest.

Presuppression and stream improvement crew. Douglas Key Renny, second from the right.

courtesy of Douglas Key Renny

John Selesky built several buildings at Higgins Lake. He served on a survey crew for ten months, working forty hours a week, from nine to five. Mr. Selesky enjoyed being responsible for his equipment and his people. Some of these fellows have become lifelong friends.

Walter Wildey erected CCC bathhouses in state parks.

George Yannett, an Odawa from the Grand Traverse Band of Chippewa and Ottawa Indians, learned to drive trucks. "In winter, I was taken off driving and put in KP, cleaning pots and pans and mopping mess hall and kitchen floors."

Leo Lamar Athey went by boat every morning from Isle Royale to Mott Island, to pack the soil with dynamite, remove the mess, and build the foundations of buildings to house equipment for the National Park Service. He also worked with jack hammers and shovels to establish a lagoon.

Nowadays, the variety of jobs assigned to one man would be called multitasking. Back then, it was just called work.

Construction

courtesy of Leo Lamar Athey

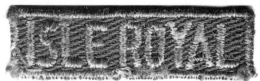

Leo Lamar Athey's old CCC patch

courtesy of Leo Lamar Athey

Getting mechanized.

courtesy of Douglas Key Renny

"We had a real chef; so on the whole, food was pretty good. It was bought locally, which boosted the economy of nearby communities. However, one day they served us beans for breakfast. This did not go down well and we were unhappy about this. One guy tipped the whole tray on the floor. The commanding officers ordered eggs for everyone. One fellow ate twenty-one!"   —Frank Munger

Lunch break at Chittenden nursery.

courtesy of Douglas Key Renny

Chester Rufus Dodge in his cook's uniform.

courtesy of Robert Dodge

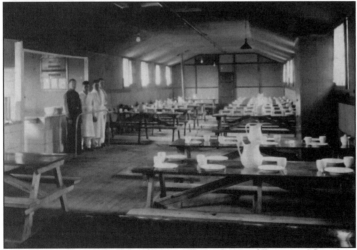

courtesy of Newaygo County Society of History and Genealogy

Mess Hall, Camp Newaygo.

Some chefs took special pride at feeding their charges. "My uncle, Wells Hall, a chef in a CCC camp for five years, loved nature and the outdoors. He always said that the Cs and he were a good match, and he prided himself on making and serving food for the boys. The Cs gave him an opportunity to earn a living without an education or diploma, and he talked about it quite often. He was an overpowering, big man with a booming voice, and a perfectionist who found faults with everyone else's cooking. I wonder how he got on with others." Anne Thatcher

Food

"I had a heck of an appetite. I actually liked 'shit on a shingle.'"
—John Selesky

Imagine an army of two hundred famished young men rushing into mess halls two to three times a day, seven days a week, ready to devour enormous helpings of hot food. Quite a daunting task for chefs, cooks, and their assistants, who had better be ready!

Very early in the morning, in all weather, men chopped wood to bank cast-iron stoves with water reservoirs and large ovens. James Fournier, a French Canadian in the Cs, had to get up early to get wood from outside. One bitter wintry day, he came back in so cold that he asked the cook to give him something to warm his insides. Cook gave him a cup of spirits with a lemony taste. Fournier swore it was almost pure alcohol, although he had never drunk liquor before. After that, his stomach burned for days, so much so that to his dying day, he never touched alcohol or anything lemony again.

While camp was still asleep, chefs and cooks and KP boys worked feverishly to cook six hundred eggs and six hundred pancakes or French toasts for breakfast. No sooner had breakfast been cleaned in the mess that ingredients for stews were chopped

[1] For the uninitiated, shit on a shingle consisted of shredded beef served on a piece of toast and topped with brown gravy or milk sauce.

courtesy of Robert Dodge

Eating in the open air.

[2] **We Can Do It** by C. Symons

and stirred in huge pots to be delivered by trucks in hot thermo containers in the woods. These were gobbled on the spot in metal kits by the 95% of the boys who worked away from camp. Lunch needed to be hot, substantial, and easy to transport on rough terrains; stews were an obvious choice. A crew of 125 enrollees at lunchtime could eat thirty-eight loaves of bread and thirty gallons of spaghetti followed by dozens of cookies and cakes, the lot washed down with forty gallons of coffee[2]. Most of the boys had not seen so much food for a long time and packed on six to over twenty pounds in weight during their first six months.

On Isle Royale, meals arrived by boat from Hancock every morning. Leo Lamar Athey, stationed on Isle Royale but working on Mott Island, remembers gulping hot, thick stew in freezing rain.

Digging and planting emptied a man's stomach pretty quickly. The 5:30 P.M. rush for dinner was astounding. An average dinner included meat, potatoes and vegetables, dessert, milk and coffee. Camps located near the Great Lakes shores managed to purchase fish from Coast Guardsmen. The occasional road kill, deer or cow, picked up by the boys or the locals, found its way into the stew. George Yannett, Odawa, Grand Traverse Band of Chippewa and Ottawa Indians, "hunted snowshoe rabbits, they're bigger than hares, and gave them to the cook who was happy to throw them in a pot." William Tylutki "enjoyed eating 'stick-to-your-ribs' food and being with kids of my own age." Stan Ward drove a food truck and, "when we had leftovers, we stopped at poor families; they knew our route and came out with pots and pans. We dished out any surplus we had."

> "While fighting a fire near Kalkaska, we had a shortage of food and had only sandwiches to eat. It did not fill our stomachs."
>
> —Edward Hartzell

courtesy of Leo Lamar Athey

Boys loved pies and were willing to do anything to get some. "Joe, our cook, wanted some blueberries to make pies and did not have the time to pick them. He shouted 'Who wants pies?' in the mess hall. The roof almost came off the place; everyone scrambled up. Pots were washed, and with three guys to a pot, we picked enough berries to make pies for over 200 of us in one hour." Gerard Perry

Rutabaga, beans, turnips, carrots, and milk were bought by wagon loads from local farmers who picked up the Cs' huge amount of kitchen garbage to feed their pigs. Kitchens were spotlessly clean, but often with inadequate refrigeration. A few veterans mentioned "blue eggs."

At first, meals were served in mess kits. When they were replaced by real plates, it made an impression on the boys. Frank Munger recorded in his diary, "February 25, 1934, we ate out of plates for the first time. We had chicken and pie."

Michael Rataj had no favorite food. "I was only too pleased to have regular meals and ate whatever was on my plate. Two hundred kids packed in a barrack were deafening. To avoid arguments, no talking was allowed during meals, just 'pass the salt, please.' In the mess hall you were taught to talk politely; language between boys can get rough, and the leaders insisted we used proper language instead of "pass me the f—g butter," which a guy uttered and would never forget. This incident reached his mother's ears, who, all her life, did not hesitate to remind him of it, even though he became a minister!

"We'd noticed that a new recruit dropped his head before eating. Someone asked, 'What are you doing?'

'Apologizing to my family for eating so much when they have nothing.' He was left alone after that."

Back in the kitchens, boys chopped, rolled, and fried non-stop all day long. Charles Crafard learned to bake bread, cakes, and pies at Higgins Lake. Clark Curry loved cooking and was sent to cooking and baking school in Wisconsin. He and his friend got the highest marks in the class. He stayed six extra weeks to complete his high school diploma.

Chefs and cooks generally knew what they were doing. However, their assistants were not always conversant with ingredients and recipes. Boys often asked, "What do I do with this

THE ONE-MEAL HUNGER STRIKE:

"One evening, we had a strike on our hands; you might call it the one-meal strike. The boys expected a full dinner, meat and potatoes after a hard day's work. They ate a huge amount of it. I worked in the kitchen and knew that meat had not been delivered in time to cook a proper meal. We scrambled to put something together. We served hotdogs. It did not sit well with the guys. They complained bitterly and refused to eat. The strike lasted one meal; the boys were famished and their stomachs rumbled. This was our only protest."

—Michael Rataj

The CCC employed real cooks, lumberjack and hotel cooks. Each of the boys had at least one week of KP. At holiday time, the boys missed their families and the CCC tried to make it up to them. Christmas and Thanksgiving dinners were sumptuous with turkeys with all the traditional trimmings. One boy, Philipps, "couldn't wait for Sundays, it was all you can eat. We did not eat gourmet food, but good, solid food, although it took me a while to eat beef heart."

or that?" Invariably the chef replied, "Throw it into the pot!" One day a boy missed a sock. Michael and coworkers looked at each other: "Oh my God!" Another time, grasshoppers kept jumping into the cooking pots and "we could not catch them all." One Thanksgiving, bags of necks and gizzards were found in several turkeys' cavities devoid of stuffing. Odd artifacts, bandages, and wood chips, were dropped in the pots unnoticed, to the surprise of their recipients.

Robert Fyvie still chuckles over the famous nut cake incident. "At the weekend, they used to show us movies in the mess hall, next to the adjacent kitchen and bake shop. The previous night, the baker had left some cake dough to rise while watching a movie. Cockroaches had gotten into the cakes and the next evening, when he served them to us in the 'movie' house, we ate them in the dark thinking they were nuts. You should have heard the crunching!"

Michael Rataj was assigned to the kitchen and mess hall and consequently gained twenty-five pounds. "We arrived undernourished; some boys put on as much as twenty-eight pounds. The reasons we all put weight on were regular meals, we did not have to worry about lack of food anymore, and we were regimented. That made us feel secure."

Education

"We got training from adults about anything we wanted to know." —Walter Wildey

Their bellies full, the boys could now turn their attention to serious endeavors or recreational activities. Many boys had only a middle-school education or had not finished high school. Twenty percent of MCCC enrollees had not completed eighth grade. A few were illiterate, their education cut short by the Great Depression and the need to find work and food. By 1934, the CCC incorporated educational programs to remedy the situation and prepare enrollees to develop pride and skills for future employment. Academic and vocational skills were offered. Illiterate boys and boys who had not graduated from high school were required to attend classes. Unemployed teachers were brought in and 90% of the MCCC boys participated in these programs. High school graduates could receive correspondence university credits for courses.

"Most of us wanted to be in class, we knew it was the chance of a lifetime. We were studious and disciplined; teach-

Michael Rataj recalled a moving story about one boy who "had only a seventh-grade education; he could hardly read or write and hated school, but he paid attention during the CCC classes. He received letters from home that one of us read for him until one day he painfully, but proudly, read one aloud to us and we all clapped."

P.C. 138650

Proficiency Certificate

THIS IS TO CERTIFY THAT _Robert E. Dodge_
of _Hart, Michigan_ while a member of C. C. C. Company
Walhalla, Michigan became proficient in _Machine Ope_
Dated _September 28, 1932_

Approved by the District Commander:
Sam H. Hill
District Educational Adviser.

CIVILIAN CONSERVATION CORPS   U.C. 1955

Unit Certificate

THIS CERTIFIES THAT _Robert E. Dodge_
Company _687_ has satisfactorily completed _15_
hours of instruction in _Auto Mechanics_
is therefore granted this Certificate.

C. F. Harden
Project Superintendent.

_____
Instructor.

_____
Company Comman

Date _12-28-39_   Place _Camp Walhal_

courtesy of Robert Dod

Proficiency
certificates

ers told us that there were "no silly questions, only questions you want answers to. And we did," said Michael Rataj. Clark Curry agrees. His ambition to become a chef came true. The Cs sent him to cooking school in Wisconsin where he obtained "the highest marks in my class and stayed on six extra weeks to get my high school diploma with honors. Thanks to all this, I was promoted at my old job when I left the Cs."

Camp educational advisors had to be resourceful and multitalented as well as be counselors and "fathers" to their young charges. They taught classes ranging from welding, typing, carpentry, cartography, drafting to university classes. This is proven by the variety of classes and skills enrollees acquired. Don Ashcroft studied First Aid and photography. Stan Ward kept trucks running and took classes on mechanics. Reverend William Elum learned to be a surveyor and earned stripes for work to "keep me away from planting trees." Ray Larson took building classes that would help him get into college after the Cs. George Yannett learned to read a compass, "later I enjoyed college, especially algebra and trigonometry."

John Selesky spoke fondly of the Cs for the self-discipline and educational opportunity. He studied

WE WANT EDUCATIONAL ADVISERS LIKE THESE, BY GUM —

courtesy of Annick Hivert-Carthew

Douglas Key Renny's first dump driving job: a '33 Dodge. Below, he got promoted and is driving a '35 GMC

theory of flight and would eventually earn his wings, and under the GI Bill, gained his commercial pilot's license. Gerard Perry was sent to Life Saving school at Perch Lake, and Marvin Bond took classes in radio, acquiring knowledge that got him more radio responsibility when he went right from the Cs into the Marines in WWII. Frank Munger "pounded a typewriter for the first time" on April 22, 1934. James Chester Underhill obtained certification in several subjects: photography, First Aid, drawing and vehicle operation.

Others brought skills to the Cs, like Douglas Key Renny who had graduated from high school where he had learned to type. He was employed as a clerk at CCC camp, which did not mean staying in an office all the time. Renny planted fish and cleaned up streams in Pere Marquette National Forest. "Once, riding in a truck convoy in very snowy conditions, one of our trucks was hit by a train. The driver did not see the train coming. No one was injured."[1] All veterans agreed that "teachers taught in an exciting way. They said that we were their best students, we were so eager to learn."

While extolling another boy's achievements Michael Rataj joked about his own lack of talent in a certain subject. "You had to take two classes while in the Cs. The problem was that my job in the mess hall ended only at 8 P.M. and my choice of classes was limited. I was told to take piano and singing lessons in the afternoon. I was not good at singing, did not have a good voice. When I asked permission to drop out, they said, 'thank you, thank you, Michael!' And that was the end of my singing career!"

[1] As told by his brother, Henry Renny

Some men hung out in the game room to see what was happening and joined groups of card and billiard players. Frank Munger spent some of his meager pocket money playing poker and recording his day in a diary. On February 4, 1934, he wrote, "We played Stud poker nearly all day. I was about 70 cents ahead."

courtesy of Newaygo County Society of History and Genealogy

Camp Newago Recreation Hall.

courtesy of Leo Lamar Athey

Playing volleyball.

Scenes from a CCC scrapbook show the enrollees occasionally took time off for fun.

courtesy of Annick Hivert-Carthew

Recreation

"I coached the boxing team and fought in the light heavyweight class. One year I came away with the 'Golden Gloves Award.'"
—John Selesky

The CCC produced several famous athletes such as Joe Louis, the "Brown Bomber" whose mighty axe swing made quite an impression. Apparently, Joe Louis kept the habit of chopping wood throughout his career.

Boxing saved Robert Fyvie's "bones." He boxed for exercise in the middleweight category in the Cs. "It was handy when I was aboard ship coming back from China during the war."

Boxing and other sports were very popular with the boys. Leaders encouraged them to participate in any kind of physical activities to "get rid of steam" and surplus energy. It's hard to believe that after a full day of firefighting and planting trees, one would have the stamina to play hard, but after a few minutes of relaxation, these spirited guys were raring to go.

William Tylutki boxed for his team in the lightweight category against fellows from other camps and from Illinois. He was knocked down by "Fuzzy Fezanatto." "I also played shortstop for my baseball team, and had more fun with that."

> "We had a lot of Golden Gloves from Detroit and Hamtramck, such as Walter Karpenscki, a heavyweight champion."
>
> —Frank Munger

"We had dancing lessons so we could go to the town dances. We practiced with each other. The 'girls' had a handkerchief tied on their arms. It was not the most popular role among us! At first we felt odd, but after learning the proper steps and becoming popular among the local girls, we got used to it."

—Michael Rataj

courtesy of Leo Lamar Athey
The one that didn't get away.

Aside from boxing, the most popular sport was baseball, followed by football. Clarence Springer played football for the camp team and competed against other camps. They had teams for everything—volleyball, swimming, wrestling—and if a team of one's favorite sport did not exist, it was quickly set up. They could fish, ice skate, play pool and ping pong.

Always gung-ho for action, teams competed within their own and against other camps. Really good teams vied for state championships in their category. Gerald McNeil pitched for the baseball team. A gleeful shine came up in his eyes when he mentioned that "we won the championship against Camp Pontiac." George Yannett played third base for the softball team that won several games against other camps and towns. "It was pure entertainment." Competing against the local community did not always improve relations. "Over the Fourth of July, we had a tug-of-war against the town of Cadillac's firemen. We pulled them so far into the lake, we were no longer welcome!" relates Cameron Glynn.

Not everyone wanted to sweat in a boxing ring or on a baseball diamond. The library was heavily frequented by boys like Don Ashcroft who preferred to read Christian and geography books. To renew their stock and provide material, camp libraries exchanged books with each other. Fellows like Douglas Key Renny were avid readers and spent most evenings at the library, reading almost any kind of books as well the Camp newspaper and *Happy Days*, the national CCC newspaper. Ray Larson pored over the local newspaper from Ironwood and the miners' paper *Pix*.

Most camps had their own newspaper. Leaders urged enrollees to participate in its writing and production. Censure hardly existed, and sometimes bawdy pieces were printed. Pieces of work that showed some insensitivity to others were not published.

Company 677, of Harrison, put together the first "tabloid," *The Daily Dip*. Enrollees could obtain two copies, one for himself and one for home. Enrollees created the name of their camp newspaper. Company 679, in Wellston, named theirs *The Hoxeyville Daze*, and Company 669, Manistique, *The Mocking Bird*. Topics varied from wit and humor, fiction writing, poetry, "hooks and jabs" corner for boxing news, and at Christmas, letters from Santa! Wit abounded. The *Peacocker*, from Peacock, described itself as, "fourth class literature, third class reading matter, second class news and first class scandal."[1]

Shooting Craps   courtesy of Leo Lamar Athey

Many guys played Craps. "I played once and lost. I thought of borrowing, but decided against it. Interest on borrowing from other boys could be as high as 100%." Gerald McNeil

[1]**The CCC Chronicles**,
Alfred Emile Cornebise

[2]**The CCC Chronicles**,
Alfred Emile Cornebise

Some papers had a "Dear Abby" style column to counsel on the "matters of the heart." Boys requested real and fake advice on love. Responses were as quirky as the questions. "I'm in love with two girls, one pretty, young and poor; the other old, ugly and very rich. Which one should I marry?" Response: "Marry the young one, send me the other."[2]

As war loomed over Europe and the U.S., and the CCC prepared boys for National Defense, more news of the conflict appeared.

In the hobby room, Michael Rataj "was taught bow and arrow making by a Native American leader. It took three months to make a nice bow; you can say it taught me patience!"

Philipps took pleasure in old-time square dancing, but did not participate in sports; he was too busy "running around downtown Ludington, where I met my wife. We went to elementary school together. I used to torment her, taking her dolls away."

"Most boys missed their moms and wrote frequently. Letters were often addressed to 'Dear Mom,' and on the last line, just above their signatures, 'by the way, how's Dad?'"

—Michael Rataj

A singing group. "In my camp we had a guy who played the guitar and sang very well, and the Drum and Bugle Corps played for us and competed against other camps." Michael Rataj

Robert Elmer Dodge was willing to sit anywhere to play anything. When not reading, Ray Larson listened to local radio programs from the Ironwood station and WLS Chicago.

Meanwhile Waldo "Red" Fisher picked on younger guys or wrote many letters home because he was homesick. Leo Lamar Athey learned to march and went through the manual of arms from front to back, a useful asset when he was drafted in 1942. Charles Crafard munched on candy bars purchased at the canteen, as did many fellows. Toward the end of the month, wallets could be empty and money was "borrowed" from other guys, sometimes at 100% interest.

Almost every camp had an orchestra that played for dances held in the mess hall and in towns close by. Camp Evelyn boasted to have the best orchestra in the Upper Peninsula.

Reverend William Elum organized a singing quartet and was the lead singer. They sang at churches and in nightclubs. Reverend Elum also went to Manistee once a month to go to the theater, sitting in the upper balcony, the only place he could afford.

CCC boys and local girls eagerly attended camp and town dances. However, most boys had never learned the proper steps or even how to invite a young lady to dance before joining the Cs.

Annually, the CCC celebrated FDR's birthday (January 30) with special activities, dances, special dinners, poems and other tributes to the President.

Barracks

"You should have heard the snoring!"
—Ray Larson

Imagine the racket of forty to sixty men in wooden barracks, or twelve men in a tent, snoring and coughing. This did not stop Robert Elmer Dodge from "sleeping very well."

[1] **We Can Do It** by C. Symons

"We went to bed at 9:30 P.M., and after two weeks, you did not hear the snoring nor Taps at 10:00 P.M. We dropped to bed, exhausted. Days were long and morning came back too quickly after eight hours of sleep." Michael Rataj

Barracks were sided with medium-weight tarpaper held on by battens and covered with Cellotex on the inside. There was some wood paneling and the wood floors had to be scrubbed by hand with brushes and G.I. soap.[1]

"Huge barracks for forty to sixty boys were divided inside in three sections. Each section looked after its own stove and had to keep it clean. You had a roster for stove, floor and bed duties, almost like the Army. Barracks were inspected by older boys who had

courtesy of Douglas Key Renny

Hanging out in the barracks on February 25, 1936. Renny's bed is in the foreground.

Left to right, hospital-bathhouse-mess hall-supply house.

After living in large "homes" and wide open spaces, several veterans mentioned feeling claustrophobic when they went back to a small bedroom in a big town or city.

courtesy of Douglas Key Renny

Below: Barracks ready for inspection.

become barrack leaders after one year in the Cs. They had to have a good rating and be good at their work and, of course, be willing to re-enlist every six months for up to two years. You could not do more than two years, too many boys were waiting." Michael Rataj

courtesy of Newaygo County Society of History and Genealogy

Reverend William Elum was promoted to barrack leader and saw to its cleanliness and orderliness. He was responsible for maintaining order, bedtime lights out, and blankets folded according to military code.

Ray Larson remembers, "the crew chief slept in a room at the head of the barrack. The blankets on our cots had to be tight enough to bounce a coin off." Larson was posted at Camp Norrie, company 3601, on the Montreal River, the borderline between Michigan and Hurley, Wisconsin.

Some camps were not established at all. "Tents were shipped; tents for bathhouse, galleys and the First Aid shack. We first cleared the land and set them up in rectangular shapes, sleeping tents far enough from latrines and galleys." Frank Munger

Life was harsher for the boys living in tents. John Gilmour and eleven other boys slept in a pyramid tent for three months. There was a small wood-burning stove that put out a little heat. "In the morning it was tough to get up when it was below zero. You should have seen the speed at which we dressed and rushed out, freezing, to do mandatory push ups and calisthenics."

Boys were responsible for chopping their own wood to feed their tent's wood-burning stove. They took turns, and the barrack leader established a roster to that effect. John Gilmour still smarts at the one enrollee who refused to get out in the cold to get the wood. The boys could not induce him to do it. The tent decided to go on strike. If this bad apple did not want to cooperate, then no one would. "After two days of -10° F weather, we were ready to chop wood, even the mutinous guy."

courtesy of Douglas Key Renny

The CCCs took time to spruce up and repair their barracks.

courtesy of Douglas Key Renny

"The CCC taught us to respect each other and work together. In fact we did everything together—work, eat, study, play ball and sleep! My three best pals were German, Polish and Italian. I never used a derogatory word again after that.

—Michael Rataj

courtesy of Douglas Key Renny

courtesy of Douglas Key Renny
Friends

"I was born in a white Anglo-Saxon Protestant community. In the CCC, I was exposed to Italians, Poles, a few blacks and Native Americans, many Germans and several Finns. All different from me, not the way I had been raised. When I was assigned to side camp, working with dynamite away from the main camp, we had an Italian guy, whom we nicknamed 'Mafia.' We became very good friends and met again in 1986 during the organization of the CCC association."

—Frank Munger

Getting Along

"There were many national rivalries, each of us thinking we were better than the others. We were a bit narrow-minded, but the CCC changed all that, forced us to get along."
—Frank Munger

"At first, the boys did not always get along together because of ethnic and racial slurs and prejudices that most of us had acquired in the cities. There were many rivalries and name-calling between the Irish, Italian, German, Polish boys, and blacks; even the Italians from the south did not get along with the Italians from the north! We used names such as 'Dagos, Krauts, Buffaloes or Niggers,' without thinking about their implication or meaning. The CCC quickly put a stop to that!

"At the beginning the CCC was not segregated; but leaders decided they had enough problems keeping ethnic groups getting along without dealing with racial disputes as well. Black CCC camps were created." Michael Rataj

Don Ashcroft reminisced that "a few guys struggled with

At ease!

courtesy of Robert Dodge

courtesy of Robert Dodge

courtesy of Leo Lamar Athey

John Selesky discovered "self-discipline and being responsible for my machines and my people. I met a lot of people in the Cs. Some became lifelong friends."

English but it was the main language spoken. Others talked in their native tongue together. We were often given nicknames—Cowboy, Horsy, Stone Face, Dud and Doc."

"My name was Lightning because I moved at a slower pace. It did not bother me; I learned to assume my responsibilities and to stand upon my word." Ray Larson

The CCC gave Reverend William Elum "leadership skills. I'd never had an opportunity to lead before. I excelled at what they let me do. It made me think more of myself because the Depression made you feel like a dog, but I wanted to learn, and the CCC was the first chance I had to do it. If I hadn't had a chance, I might have rebelled and ended up in jail."

Marvin Bond and Arthur Barnes developed the ability to deal with other people.

So did Reverend William Elum, who did not drink or smoke or fight and kept a clear head. "The CCC taught me how to work with others and made me aware of the way people treated and thought of each other, good or bad, and that knowledge has stuck with me. I have learned from both, the good and bad, a useful tool, especially in my ministry when dealing with conflict."

When he became a leader, Gerard Perry "found out that I could deal with anybody." In the short time he was in the Cs, Edward Hartzell (who cheated on his age, fifteen and a half instead of seventeen, and was sent back home), "found out how to get on in the world and go somewhere."

Clark Curry was the only black kid at cooking school and was made fun of. "I was quick-tempered, it could have lead me into trouble, but my teacher took me aside to say, 'You must subdue your passion, because these guys want to hurt mentally.'"

Elmer Leach stated "there was the occasional bully, but no more than usual. I wasn't a problem kid, kind of shy."

A few made lasting friendships, like Philipps who "did not have too many friends, just one or two people hanging together," and still sees one of them, or John Selesky who made lifelong friends that he met at the CCC camp.

Others were busy, inhaling life to the fullest. George Yannett, Odawa, Grand Traverse Band of Chippewa and Ottawa Indians, "had lots of good friends, good food and proper training. The leaders were good. I was never lonely, too much excitement, everything was too interesting."

courtesy of Leo Lamar Athey

Smiling fellows enjoying 'the kind of life you wished for, and got it,' according to William Tylutki.

courtesy of Leo Lamar Athey

"I learned to help my guys develop, cooperate and prepare for the future. Everyone got along, regardless of how different."

—Cameron Glynn

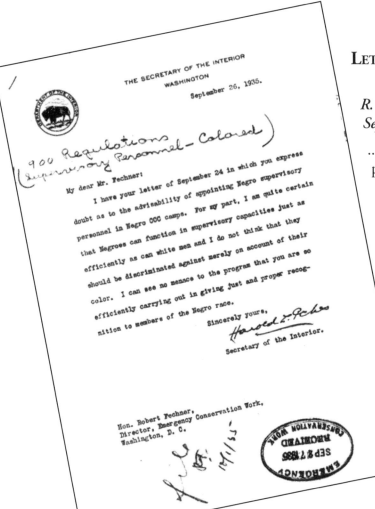

R. Fechner to Thomas L. Griffith, 21 Sept. 1935

..."While segregation has been the general policy, it has not been inflexible, and we have a number of companies containing a small number of negro enrollees. I am satisfied that the negro enrollees themselves prefer to be in companies exclusively of their own race.

"This segregation is not discrimination and cannot be so construed. The negro companies are assigned the same type of work, have identical equipment, are served the same food, and have the same quarters as white enrollees."

Harold Ickes to Robert Fechner, 26 Sept. 1935

..."For my part, I am quite certain that negroes can function in supervisory capacities just as efficiently as can white men and I do not think that they should be discriminated against merely on account of their race."

FDR to Robert Fechner, 27 Sept 1935

"In the CCC Camps, where boys are colored, in the Park Service work, please try to put in colored foremen, not of course in technical work but in the ordinary manual work."

Robert Fechner to Robert J. Bulkley, 4 June 1936

..."Whether we like it or not, we cannot close our eyes to the fact that there are communities and states that do not want and will not accept A Negro Civilian Conservation Corps Company. This is particularly true in localities that have a negligible Negro population."

African Americans in the CCC

"The CCC changed me positively. I discovered that I had leadership ability. I had never had a chance to lead before."
—Reverend William Elum

"At first the CCC was not segregated. Fellows were assigned to camps without regard to race or ethnicity. My camp was integrated; a mixture of several nationalities and races did everything together. Unfortunately, some of us were quite ignorant; name calling and rivalries between different nationalities often arose. The Cs quickly put a stop to that. I never used a derogatory word after the Cs.

"Not everyone reacted the way I did. We had a few hard heads, not just in my camp, but all over the nation. Leaders decided they had enough problems keeping ethnic groups getting along without dealing with racial disputes as well. Officials agreed and segregated

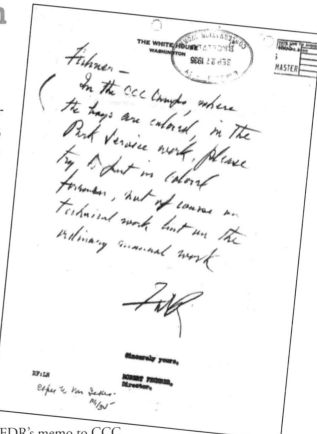

FDR's memo to CCC Director Robert Fechner.

courtesy of Rainelle Burton

Bonner Burton

Bonner Burton had a rough time in a segregated camp. "When my father was laid off from Bud Wheels, he enrolled in the CCC. It was not a pleasant experience. Leaders were white but workers black. He felt alienated. However he was not bitter. He said that it gave him an appreciation of different degrees of work and how to transform working under adversarial conditions into a positive experience."

—Rainelle Burton, daughter of Bonner Burton

camps were created despite an earlier ban against segregation and discrimination." Michael Rataj

The first all-black company in Michigan was put together at Camp Custer in 1933, and then sent to Camp Mack Lake.

Regardless of segregation, African Americans with special skills were sometimes assigned to white companies in need of their talents. According to Frank Munger, Camp Custer "had two or three African Americans. They ate, worked and relaxed with us, except they slept in their own tent."

Several African American veterans preferred the company of other blacks while others worked and socialized with whites, given that they shared the same CCC experience. Arthur Barnes did not have any problems mixing with whites, but sought out the company of blacks by affinity.

Black and white veterans agreed that African American companies and black individuals excelled in sport competitions, especially in boxing, where many became champions, such as Joe Louis.

By 1935, the CCC had remedied the white leaders/black enrollees situation. Most camps had black advisers acting as counselors and mediators when conflict erupted between enrollees and personnel. In 1941, 2,000 "colored" project assistants' leaders and assistant leaders were on duty at CCC Camps. Nationally, 900 classes in "Negro History" were conducted in the camps during 1935-41.[1]

Clark Curry benefited from his educational adviser's counsel. While in the CCC, Curry finished high school and graduated at the top of his class at a baking and cooking school in Wisconsin, where the Cs had sent him upon his request. He was the only black kid in the camp, an oddity. A young white fellow who became his best friend had never seen a black man before. Being the only black kid among so many whites created some teasing (not always of the nice kind). Curry was "a quick-tempered youth." His adviser took him aside to urge him to "subdue his passion and quick temper."

Then came the day Clark Curry's sense of justice got the better of him. A white leader requested some breakfast. Curry cooked as well as he had been taught to do, and placed a plate in front of the leader, not noticing a drop of

[1]Washington, D.C.: United States Printing Offices, 1941

The real problem lay with the police. There were very few African Americans in the area; we were a rarity and therefore were often under suspicion of misconduct. If they saw you walking, they'd arrest you even if you did not do anything wrong.

—Reverend William Elum

courtesy of Annick Hivert-Carthew

Reverend William Elum with interviewer Jessica DeMink Carthew at the 2005 MCCC annual reunion

Working together

grease on its edge. It was only tiny, but, "The guy showed no mercy on me and hit the roof. 'Go and clean up this plate,' he ordered. Infuriated and hurt, Curry told him to 'take the plate and fix it yourself.' I did not care if he had bars on his shoulders; I was not going to let another man abuse me." Clark Curry requested a leave of absence, took the last train to Detroit and never returned to camp. The next day he got his old job back at Bud Wheel.

For the record, no more disciplinary problems occurred in black camps than in white ones.

Reverend William Elum, a Detroit boy who adjusted well to working in the wilderness, found the CCC people nicer than city folks and, "Camp was less crowded than an urban environment, and I breathed fresh air." All of his work mates were black, officers white. "People in the camp got along pretty well. In any case, I did not drink or smoke or fight, and kept a cool head. The real problem lay with the police. There were very few African Americans in the area; we were a rarity and therefore were often under suspicion of misconduct. If they saw you walking, they'd arrest you even if you did not do anything wrong. Camp director would come and get us out. It happened to my buddies and me. We were arrested walking along a road. Someone had stolen a car, not we. We stayed over-night in jail although we kept telling them we were innocent. In White Cloud, Manistee, you had to mind your p's and q's." That did not stop Reverend Elum from singing in bars and churches in a quartet he'd put together, nor attending the local theater, in the upper balcony, where it was cheap. He went by CCC trucks.

Black and white enrollees could rise in rank through dili-

"The CCC taught me to deal with people. CCC allowed me to do things for other people that they could not do themselves."
—Clark Curry

gence, as did Reverend Elum who earned stripes for good work and became a surveyor and a barrack leader. "I excelled at what the CCC let me do and I began to think more positively of myself because the Depression had made me feel like a dog. I wanted to learn and improve myself. The CCC gave me that first chance."

By 1938, the economy showed some signs of improvement; white boys began to find jobs outside the CCC. Not so for black ones. In fact black enrollees tended to remain longer in the Cs than white ones for this reason. Walter White, executive secretary of the NAACP, recommended that Cs significantly increase the percentage of black enrollees in the program. It was rejected. With the approach of war, black and white camps were gradually eliminated at the same rate. By the end of 1942, all were closed.

The Trojan was produced monthly at Company 2694, of Harrison, Michigan. "Camp Houghton Lake, Camp Bitely, and Camp Stronach were expected to contribute a display to the '73 years of Negro Progress Exposition' in Detroit, May 10-19...One enrollee from the three companies would be selected to accompany the exhibit."

The crew of Camp Marquette just out from dinner
February 22, 1935.

courtesy of Marquette County Historical Society

Camp
Marquette's
parade float,
1935.

courtesy of Marquette County Historical Society

Native Americans in the CCC

"I was never lonely in the Cs; too much excitement, everything was too interesting—lots of good friends, good food and proper training." —George Yannett, Odawa, Grand Traverse Band of Ottawa & Chippewa Indians

More than 3,000 Native Americans worked at Camp Marquette, west of Sault Ste Marie in Chippewa County. The U.S. Forest Service and the U.S. Bureau of Indian Affairs established the camp on the Marquette National Forest specifically for Native Americans, the only one in the nation.

Rules differed from other camps. Enrollment was more liberal. Local and out-of-state Native Americans were accepted, sometimes as "walk-in," and as old as forty-five. There was no food budget restriction and recruits did not always wear CCC garb for work; they were also given practical civilian clothing more suitable to their work and the harsh climate conditions.

Recruits represented almost any trade. They were on the whole very qualified and worked so diligently that the Forest Service judged Camp Marquette one of its best camps.

Some fellows went home on leave; Yannett did not. "Why should I have depended on my folks for a few days when they had nothing?"

Camp Marquette recruits laying the subfloor of St. Mary's Hospital. courtesy of Marquette County Historical Society

Camp Marquette worked on many projects—roads, bridges, rearing ponds construction, forest and land improvement.

Due to the older ages of the CCC Native Americans, locating veterans for interview in preparation for this book proved difficult. Fortunately, George Yannett, an Odawa from the Grand Traverse Band of Chippewa and Ottawa Indians, responded to my call.

A fellow Ottawa recruited Yannett at sixteen. He was glad to leave home. He'd been raised on a "bitty" farm with pigs and horses. He was poor and unemployed and immediately "liked what the CCC was doing, planting trees where there was devastation, and fighting soil erosion. FDR and his programs were popular with us.

"Leaders were good, a mixture of white and Native Americans. I wanted to become one, but was too young. To tell the truth, I was too busy enjoying life, good food and friends, going to town to play tricks on the girls to impress them, and drinking beer at the local tavern. While I had a great time with the Cs, the nearby community tolerated us only because we brought trade to them."

Young Yannett had seen forest fires before entering the Cs, but only from a distance. Foresters trained his unit for fire-fighting. "I was given a spade and a hoe, and never thought I could get hurt. The spades were heavy to work with, made of cast iron and steel. At first, everyone had blisters, then calluses. We carved our initials on our spade because our hands got used to its feel and we wanted to hang on to the same one. "

Learning came easy to Yannett; he took advantage of the on-site training to learn to drive gravel trucks and read a compass. "In winter I was taken off driving and put in KP, washing pots and pans, mopping mess hall and kitchen. Sometimes I hunted snowshoe rabbits and handed them to the cook who was happy to fix them."

In his spare time Yannett played pool, ping pong and third base for the camp softball team's competition against other camps and towns.

Odawa George
Yannett in 2005.

courtesy of Annick Hivert-Carthew

Yannett sighed. "As a Native American, I was treated better in the CCC than now, here, in the Grand Traverse Bay, or in the Army. I wish they'd continue the CCC; we need it for all young people."

One Native American is reported to have observed that "The white man stole our land in the first place, cut off the timber, and now they are making us plant it again."[1]

"They were tolerant in the Cs, but in the Army, it was a different story. They assumed that because I was a Native American, I knew nothing. The CCC taught me not to be sloppy, to do the job correctly the first time."

—George Yannett

[1]**You Can Do It!** Charles A. Symon, page 78.

A CCC scrapbook depicts one form of discipline.

DID <u>YOU</u> EVER RUN THE GAUNTLET?

WHACK-

courtesy of Annick Hivert-Carthew

"If enrollees misbehaved, MPs kept them in jail until midnight, then back to camp for KP."

—Cameron Glynn

"There was no conflict in my camp except a couple of organized boxing matches in winter to get rid of our surplus of energy. We had a few troublemakers who did not stay long. One fellow was sent home because he was too lonely and cried all the time. I did what I was told, never got into trouble."

—Frank Munger

courtesy of Douglas Key Renny

Sawing firewood, extra duty for a minor infraction.

Discipline

"When you're eighteen or nineteen, no one can tell you nothin'." —Clark Curry

Some recruits arrived at camp with a swaggering attitude. Despite this outward behavior, discipline in the camps was not a major problem. According to Waldo "Red" Fisher, "Kids who were headed for trouble saw right away that there was no place for it in the Cs."

"We were sent as far from home as possible; there were less chances to get away, there was no escape. We were stuck! Only three boys ran away, could not hack it, one came back. The CCC sent you a train ticket to return to camp. Return escapees were accepted again, but had to pay for the folly by moving wood piles from here to there and doing KP." Michael Rataj

When a problem arose, the Army regulations took care of it. Offenders rarely received severe disciplinary action; most of the time, they were admonished to "straighten out," or given a reprimand with extra KP duty or some other mild punishment.

Although the Army ran the camps, enrollees were civilians. There were no guard houses, and no need to salute the captains.

"Depending on the severity of the offense you had to clean the kitchen grease pots with a short spoon. After punishment, everyone teased you a little, and then it was forgotten. You felt foolish and never did it again."

—Michael Rataj

Reverend William Elum obeyed the rules and stayed out of in trouble. "Tight structure was very good if you did not rebel and if you wanted 'to know.' I did not drink or smoke or fight and kept a clear head." Robert Fyvie followed his dad's advice, "Dad told me 'the way to win a fight is to stay out of it.' It worked for me." George Yannett says, "I was very young and did what I was told."

However, strict discipline and regimentation applied. Now and then some boys could not "hack it" and "got kicked out because they went 'over the hill,'"[1] says Robert Elmer Dodge. They could not be forced to return to camp or go to jail, but desertion went on their record and they were "dishonorably discharged."

Ray Larson felt very strongly about sticking to the Cs. "I had made a commitment to the Cs. It would not have been right to run away."

AWOL was treated differently. A few incidences occurred where boys went home on leave and missed a train back or were a couple of days late due to inclement weather. They were charged one or two days AWOL on their record and could still be honorably discharged. Robert Elmer Dodge obtained a weekend leave and "walked all the way from Walhalla and the ferry" and made sure to get back on time.

The Cs treated bad behavior and delinquency seriously. Thieves, hard heads and petty criminals were dismissed.

In winter, when the boys could be cooped up in barracks by snow for several days, a few brawls erupted, generally ending up with bath duty or grease-pots cleaning for the culprits.

Officers knew how to defuse disputes. "One time a buddy was fighting with another recruit. The sergeant stopped them and said that he would arrange a fight so they could settle their argument. The next night, the sergeant postponed it because of paperwork, the next one because of some emergency. And when finally he said that the fight was on, the guys did not want fight any more." Michael Rataj

Troubled boys were encouraged to unload their problems to the camp chaplain and educational advisers whose positions included counseling. In some camps, enrollees established kangaroo courts to settle matters themselves. Philipps and his buddies took action when a "fellow never washed. He was so filthy; I swear his uniform could stand up on its own. One day we ganged up on him and threw him in the water and scrubbed him until his clothes fell off and his skin was bright red. Years later, I saw the same guy in the Army and he was still dirty."

There were a few rebellions. In one incident, "The whole camp went on strike. The CCC did not pay us on time. The camp rebelled. The 'top kick' notified the commanding officer living in Rapid River and got him to come back to camp. Lieutenant Price, a graduate from West Point, arrived with his .45 strapped around his waist and whistled for everyone to come out. He pulled the two ringleaders by the scruff of the neck in the middle of the assembly and said, 'You will go to work.' And the camp did. My tent did not go on strike. When it happened we were on KP and missed it all." Frank Munger

MPs discouraged teasing. "I was making fun of one of my buddies on punishment duty, painting huge numbers on the water tower with a one-inch brush. The captain heard me and handed me a one-inch brush too. My friend and I spent a lot of time painting these numbers!" Michael Rataj

"One little smoke before going back to duty."

"Did I do anything wrong?"

A. Lecuyer and C. Lavelle, posing for the camera.

One instance of teasing tragically led to suicide. "A fellow in camp had weak kidneys. Someone found out that his mattress was rotten. Guys made a bit of fun of him. He was so ashamed that he walked to the railroad tracks and let a train roll over him. There was no teasing after that." William Tylutki

All in all veterans agreed that camp leaders, although strict, understood boys quite well and generally showed tolerance and a good sense of humor.

Nevertheless, by 1939, one boy out of five deserted at considerable cost to the Cs that had fed, clothed, and trained him. A committee spent four years to establish the causes of this high desertion rate. It concluded that as the economy had picked up, the "best" boys found jobs and did not need the CCC, and that the new enrollees, per force, were of "lesser" quality than before. America watched Hitler's moves in Europe, and was getting ready for a possible war. The Army recalled more qualified officers and put inferior or inadequately prepared ones in their

"The flag was always there to remind us that we worked for our country and that any misconduct cast a shadow on the CCC." Leo Lamar Athey

"I don't even want to think what would have happened to me if I had not joined. I was stealing, mixing with a bad crowd, and was always in trouble. The CCC straightened me out, there was no room for me to get into trouble. I was away from my toxic environment. All my adult life I paid back what the CCC, the LEMs, and forestry people gave me: they showed me how to do things right. I was a scout master for twenty-five years and applied more or less the same practices as the CCC."

—Michael Rataj

place, thereby creating more problems for the Cs. The youths were rougher and less willing to put up with discomfort. The officers were ineffectual in quelling mutinies and desertions.

The CCC sincerely endeavored to find solutions to this problem, but it had been created as a response to poverty and social problems, a reputation that worked against it as it tried to compete for employees with the private sector. It tried to change this image, but young men preferred not to belong to a program that was still viewed as a relief agency.

Physical Health

"March 10, 1934. I am learning the ropes pretty fast in First Aid. We are treating about seven fellows with lacerations of the feet and hands." —Frank Munger's diary

Before joining the Cs, recruits were examined and inoculated. Quite a few of them suffered from malnutrition. After a few weeks of good, healthy food, fresh air and regular exercise, starting with mandatory early morning calisthenics, young men gained weight and became healthier and stronger.

At camp, doctors and orderlies practiced routine examinations and treated minor diseases and injuries. Don Ashcroft testified that "I had an accident once, and the doctor took good care of me."

The medical officer served as leader and oversaw the camp sanitary conditions and made sure they were maintained. Camp Paradise had a bad case of the "runs." There were not enough toilets to accommodate everyone. Boys dug holes all over the area.[1]

Ray Larson was grateful for the infirmary! "I came back from the town of Hurley with my friend after drinking too much 'Dago Red', a cheap Italian wine made of Dago grapes. I woke up in the dispensary sicker than a dog."

"Most camps had a resident doctor and two orderlies on duty at all times. At mine, we had a First Aid room with four beds. No money was taken away for sick days."

—Michael Rataj

[1] Charles Symon, **You Can Do It!**

BRING ME MY CLEAVER —
HE HAS FALLEN ARCHES —
WE MUST OPERATE

HUH —

YOU BETTER BE CAREFUL
OR "DOC" WILL GET YOU !

courtesy of Annick Hivert-Carthew

[2] Charles Symon, **You Can Do It!**

courtesy of Leo Lamar Athey

A few weeks of hard physical labor and the boys grew stronger.

"We suffered mostly from cuts and scratches on our feet and fingers. Inexperienced fellows sliced their shoes with sharp axes. More serious injuries were rushed to the nearest hospital." William Tylutki

Orderlies were plucked by a camp captain without much warning or training. "The camp doctor told me to give Castor Oil to anyone who complained of a stomachache. Generally it worked well, but one morning this fellow, suffering from a stomachache, came to see me. I gave him the usual dose of Castor Oil. He came back in the afternoon, feeling much worse, 'My stomach is killing me,' he said. I called the doctor who drove him to Munising Hospital. He had a perforated appendix. Thank goodness he survived! Another time, I had to call the doctor to stitch a one-inch gap in a fellow's neck he'd cut swinging an axe." Frank Munger

Misfortune did occur; there were deaths from illnesses and accidents. Young men could be reckless and feel infallible; they sometimes handled dynamite carelessly and drove too fast, and firefighting took its toll on the recruits. "Two enrollees were killed in Camp Au Train when a case of dynamite they were handling on a road project exploded."[2]

Poignant tragedies took place. Gerard Perry will never forget "The day one fellow died under my watch. I found him still in bed during a barrack inspection. 'What's wrong? If you're sick you should report to the dispensary.' He did not go. A few hours later, when I checked on him again, his skin had a yellow tint. We called the doctor who told us to bring him immediately to the hospital. The next day he died around noon.

"I was sent to meet with the body and to take it back to the fellow's mother. I took with me three guys from

Leo Lamar Athey recorded in his photo album that "Today, Manez Gonzales died." Athey was stationed on Isle Royale. "Manez woke up one morning with tremendous pain in his groin. We had no doctor and no medicine and wanted to take him by boat to Hancock, but he died before anything could be done.

"When it happened, we all grew quiet. It threw a blanket on everything. You suddenly realized that it could happen to you tomorrow."

At right: the front yard with the flag at half mast for Manez Gonzales.

courtesy of Leo Lamar Athey

the area of the deceased. We had no money and went to borrow $5 from the captain. He reached in his pocket, pulled out a fiver and said, 'I will pay for it.'"

Douglas Key Renny avoided tragedy by a hair. "One of our trucks was hit by a train. The driver did not see it coming through a snow blizzard. No one was injured!"

Gerard Perry, then a young orderly, handled a challenging case with pluck and humor. "We had been snowbound for several days when a fellow was rushed in the medical building with his big toe split in two by an axe. There was no access to the camp and the doctor could not come. The medics told me to do what I could to save his toe. I decided to sew that thing up, and shot the kid with Novocain. Twenty-eight stitches later, the toe was repaired.

"Eleven days later, the doctor finally came, behind a snow plow after bribing its drivers with fresh doughnuts to plow the entire camp. He looked at the fellow's toe and exclaimed, 'Sergeant, you did a great job, sewing that toe up. Where did you learn to do this?'

"'I used to be a taxidermist,' I replied."

Left to right, hospital, bathhouse and mess hall.

courtesy of Douglas Key Renney

INTO THE SUNSET

Published in the NACCCA journal, February 2003. Read by Dr. D. Herder in his eulogy of Reverend Bill Fraser. Reverend Fraser requested it to be included because "This pretty much captures how I think and work. Its message captures the spirit of millions of us CCC boys who learned to work, focus, and get things done while we were in the camps."

Let me die, working.
Still tackling plans unfinished, tasks undone!
Clean to its end, swift may my race be run.
No laggard steps, no faltering, no shirking:
Let me die working!

Let me die, thinking.
Let me fare forth still with an open mind,
Fresh secrets to unfold, new truths to find.
My soul undimmed, alert, no questions blinking:
Let me die thinking!

Let me die, laughing.
No sighing o'er past sins, they are forgiven.
Spilled on this earth are all the joys of heaven.
The wine of life, the cup of mirth quaffing.
Let me die laughing!

Let me die, giving.
No gloating over my gains though dearly won,
But finding joy in sharing, like God's son.
Yielding my all, ungrudged, in selfless living.
Let me die giving!

Let me die, aspiring.
Still pressing onward to obtain the prize,
Viewing the future with expectant eyes,
In labors for the Kingdom never tiring.
Let me die aspiring."

—Author unknown

courtesy of Leo Lamar Athey
The CCC gave
Leo Lamar Athey a
strong work ethic.

Spiritual Health

"No matter which way the wind is blowing, if you set your sails in the right direction, you will get there." —Johnnie Johnston, a veteran from Chapter 163 in Detroit[1]

New recruits' morale sometimes sunk low when they first arrived at camp. At the beginning of the Cs, no real religious program existed. The boys' only spiritual support came from nearby community ministers who tried their best, but did not know them well or ill-understood the Cs' lifestyle. It attracted only a few boys. "I did not participate although they trucked us to various churches." Frank Munger

By 1935 the Army endeavored to nurture the spiritual and mental needs of dejected or troubled youths. It employed a variety of full-time chaplains to counsel "down in the dumps" fellows. CCC chaplains understood their problems better than outsiders and were more successful at guiding them through crisis.

For Wayne Hamilton and many others, camp was a "safe home, some place to stay." Chaplains took it upon themselves to keep it that way.

[1] **Camp Forgotten-The Civilian Corps in Michigan,** A PBS documentary on DVD by William Jamerson

courtesy of Leo Lamar Athey

Isle Royale, isolated in Lake Superior. It took strong minds and camaraderie to endure the loneliness.

courtesy of Leo Lamar Athey

"A strong bond of camaraderie developed between recruits. The CCC became their 'family.' They were each other's support."

Corps camaraderie and spirituality affected some boys more than others. Bill Fraser, who later became a minister, embraced the camp's religious openness. "When we accept the challenge of a positive project, work together for the good of our CCC philosophy, we attract others to our fold. Working together makes others thirsty to belong." Reverend Bill Fraser, **Thoughts From a CCC Chaplain**

Young William Elum did not know yet that he would become a preacher like his father. He just knew that he "accepted The Lord in my life." Today, Reverend Elum credits the leadership skills he acquired in the Cs for helping him in his ministry. Reverend Elum devoted his life to building a church and school in Ecorse.

Chaplains held devotional services at least once a week for boys of whatever faith who attended on a voluntary basis. Douglas Key Renny attended Presbyterian services; he was from a Scottish family. Don Ashcroft read Christian books, religious articles and church reports.

On Isle Royale, Leo Lamar Athey had a chaplain who took care of all the services, "not one in particular."

"There never were too many worshippers that responded to the invitation of the good father. Yet Father Jones was a good friend to all of us."

—Reverend Bill Fraser

Clark Curry "owes much of his determination and faith in himself to the CCC." After the Cs, Curry had a life-threatening truck accident that left him paralyzed for eight months. He could not even hold his head up and worked hard every day to regain movement with the same tenacity the Corps had taught him. Curry eventually recovered. "That is the way I still am today. I may try and fail, but will find another way to do it."

Reverend Fraser passed away in 2003, but not before returning to the Cs what he got out of it. He served as the Chaplain for the National Association of Civilian Conservation Corps Alumni (NACCCA) for twelve years and wrote "Chaplain's Corner" articles for the NACCCA monthly journal. In 2000, these were culled into a book, **Thoughts From a CCC Chaplain**. He often told friends and members of his church congregations that he learned a lot about motivation in the CCC.[2]

[2] NACCCA Journal, February 2003,"A Celebration of the Life of Rev. William H. Fraser," eulogy by Dale Herder, Ph.D.

Politicians expressed their faith in official statements and speeches to the CCC. Near death in 1939, Robert Fechner, devoted director of the organization, sent members of the CCC the following Christmas message from his hospital bed. "I only wish it were possible for me to talk to each of you in person at this season of the year, when all of us look resolutely toward the future and derive renewed inspiration from the life of HIM whose birthday we commemorate on Christmas Day." Fechner died a few days later. CCC boys carried his coffin at his funeral.

courtesy of Leo Lamar Athey

After a while, unloading goods and getting news from the mainland turned into an event.

On a happy note, camp chaplains occasionally married CCC boys to their local sweethearts.

Many boys grew into spiritual men, with the typical CCC sense of humor as shown in Frank Munger's address in the NACCCA 2004 journal issue, "God grant me the senility to forget the people I never like anyway. The good fortune to run into the ones I do, and the eyesight to tell the difference."

And when death comes upon fellow alumni, the "boys" gather together to express feelings and memories.

courtesy of Leo Lamar Athey

LOOKIE, LOOKIE, LOOKIE-HERE COMES COOKIE

HOTCHA DANCES in THE C.C.C. ARE FUN

courtesy of Annick Hivert-Carthew

A CCC scrapbook depicts socializing with the local ladies.

Every Saturday night CCC fellows piled into trucks to go to town. Once there, the boys made a beeline for the nearest movie theater, bar or dance hall. "No liquor was allowed in the camp. Boys went to town to drink some. Sometimes they bought extra bottles of beer and jumped off the truck on the way back to bury them in the woods." Michael Rataj

Local and CCC boys did not always see eye to eye, especially when it came to dancing and girls. Locals did not like their girlfriends dancing with CCC boys. "We had some fights at some of the dances. Local boys tried to lick us, but they never made it. Girls waved at us in the truck. Locals didn't like it."

—Philipps

According to Douglas Key Renny, "There was lots of snow during the winter of '35-'36. At times, going to town was too much effort. Not everyone liked dancing and drinking. Curling up with a book or playing cards was appealing too."

courtesy of Douglas Key Renny

Going to town

"I was not too interested in dancing; couldn't follow the music."
—Gerald McNeil

It was not without some suspicion that folks saw two hundred boys move close to their community, especially since most of them were teenagers. By all accounts the boys were not received with open arms. Misconception and prejudice prevailed. Were they delinquents or good-for-nothings?

One factor eventually sweetened the presence of the CCC. "The community did not accept us in the beginning. They took a dim view of the CCC; they feared we would interfere with their local affairs, until they noticed their economy going up; boys bought supplies and spent money there." Frank Munger

"The nearby community tolerated us only because we brought trade to them," said George Yannett about Camp Marquette, the only camp reserved for Native Americans.

Indeed, the CCC was good for the local industry. Camps needed tools and food supplies, the boys spent what little money they had, and LEMs were recruited in the vicinity. Still, folks eyed them with some misgiving. If the situation was uncomfortable for white boys, it was worse for black ones. Several African American veterans complained of being arrested by the police as they walked, minding their own business. Many camps were in isolated places where neither the community nor the police were familiar with

"At first the community expected trouble from us, a bunch of 'wild kids.' They did not know how to take us, but it did not take them long to realize that we were well-behaved. We'd been taught good manners, to take our hat off when in female company."

—Michael Rataj

courtesy of Leo Lamar Athey

Payroll day; time to give back borrowed money, buy candy and cigarettes, and go to town.

Recruits arrived at camp completely broke. They earned $30 a month, $25 of which were automatically sent to their family. That left them with only $5. Upon arrival, the Cs gave them coupons for toothpaste and other basic necessities and charged 50 cents for a metal trunk to store their personal belongings. Only $2.50 remained in their pockets by the time they'd paid for everything. "The first few months you were left with no money and you borrowed at as high as 100% interest!"

—Michael Rataj

them. They'd be put in jail until someone from the Cs rushed to rescue them.

Everything cost money: a laundry lady to press mandatory pleats in their pants and shirts or the lease of an iron from a fellow recruit at a high interest. "It was the survival of the fittest. If you borrowed two dollars before payday, you paid back three dollars or more." William Tylutki

Boys used their wit and skills to supplement their income. Douglas Key Renny made some extra money by painting fellows' names on lockers. Frank Munger, who'd been a barber apprentice, cut hair for ten cents. The future Reverend William Elum headed and sang in a quartet that performed in churches and nightclubs so he could go to the theater in Manistee once a month. Gerard Perry played the guitar. A bartender offered him a deal: "Put a band together and you'll have as much free beer as you want." He did, and their glasses were never empty—the owner's daughter took care of them. One free drinking session remains in Gerard Perry's memory: the Hunters' Ball. He and his band buddies passed out. Perry woke up with over $100 tips in his pockets and on his chest!

Money, whatever they had, was spent on pleasurable activities. Leo Lamar Athey bought "cigarettes and candy bars—Snickers, Milky Ways—big favorite with the boys." Elmer Leach went to West Branch to see movies and roller skate. Wayne Hamilton confessed that "most of us went to town to drink beer and get friendly with local girls."

"Saturday nights in Hurley, lumberjacks made bets with each other to see how far they could go, up one side of the street and down the other, having a drink in each saloon. Sooner or later they got drunk and indulged into free-for-all fights. Indians from the reservation joined in these fights. It was a busy night at Ironwood Hospital with knife wounds! Occasionally bodies were found floating in the Montreal River on Sunday morning."[1]

Recruits did not have to go to town to get drunk. At times, alcohol reached them in the middle of the woods. To this day, Frank Munger does not drink very much, not after his team, on a side site, "bought a gallon of some alcoholic drink from a local bootlegger. It was so powerful that the next day, when we woke up, it was like walking on stilts!"

Drinking and dancing did not appeal to everyone. Douglas Key Renny was a mild-mannered type of guy who stayed that way all of his life. The LEM who'd taken him under his wing had a car, a coupe for three passengers, and took him for rides.

Michael Rataj told a story that illustrates the misunderstanding between CCC boys and communities; it involves black recruits and a white family.

"I heard of an incident with fifteen black guys who were sent to fight forest fires on a regular basis. They were the most polite guys you'd ever meet. Each day, at the same hour, their trucks passed in front of an isolated farmhouse owned by a white woman with several children who played in the front yard.

"Fifteen minutes before their expected passage she used to call in her children. She was afraid of the fifteen black youths until one day, a CCC boy noticed flames and smoke coming out of the outhouse close to the house. He yelled for the driver to stop. The guys jumped out, extinguished the fire, and saved the family from disaster. Every Sunday after that the boys had a standing invitation to have dinner at the farm."

Ray Larson confided that "most Saturdays we went to the town of Hurley, Wisconsin, a mile away from us. Within four blocks they were eighty-one saloons with prostitutes and gambling. We never had any money for any of that but we watched the miners and lumberjacks do it."

[1]based on Ray Larson, **The Larsons**, page 44

courtesy of Leo Lamar Athey

All's quiet on Isle Royale. You needed to take a boat to go to Hancock.

"Jazz dancing is degrading. It lowers all the moral standards...The lower nature is stirred up as a prelude to unchaperoned adventure." —J.R. MacMahon, "Unspeakable Jazz Must Go!" The Ladies' Home Journal, December 1921

One CCC scrapbook encouraged men to honor their fellow recruits.

'TWAS GOOD BYE ON THE ISLE OF CAPREE

BEST SINGER
PASTE KODAK HEADS ON FIGURES

courtesy of Annick Hivert-Carthew

Finding a new friend in the spring.

courtesy of Douglas Key Renny

"The Corps taught us to respect women and have good manners with them. We were quite popular with the girls and that miffed a few local boys. One day, as we were approaching town in our truck, an officer at the wheel, a boy whistled at a girl and shouted at her in an inappropriate way. The driver reported him and he was punished for 'bringing shame to the Cs and humiliating the girl.' He was told to 'respect ladies.' When he replied, 'How do I know she is a lady?' The answer was, 'From now on, every girl is a lady to you; do you understand?'"

—Michael Rataj

Girls, Love, and Money

"I did not have a girlfriend. It was too expensive; you had to have money to take a girl out on a date. We'd go to the Iron Drum in Ironwood, where they had skating downstairs and dancing upstairs."
—Ray Larson

lcohol and women were forbidden in camps. That did not stop boys from dreaming about them. Liquor, they obtained quite easily; girls were another story. They were often chaperoned or dated local boys; dates were too expensive for the recruits' limited funds.

CCC boys' sentiment over women was a bit confused. On one hand they idealized glamorous Hollywood women such as Ginger Rogers and Mae West, and on the other they showed quite an anti-women perspective, especially in camp newspapers. Rough vernacular went as far as calling dancing with girls "hog wrestling." In spite of this, "Girls would come from Grand Rapids, Muskegon. Men loved them girls! But I was not raised like that." Reverend William Elum

The CCC discouraged sexist attitudes and encouraged good manners. The Cs recommended the boys read **The West Point Manual of Courtesies and Customs of the Service**, as well as Emily Post's **Etiquette in Society, in Business, in Politics, and at Home.**

courtesy of Annick Hivert-Carthew

courtesy of Douglas Key Renny

Camps adopted pets; they were less expensive than girls, and no one fought over them.

Reverend Bill Fraser fell in love with his future bride in a restaurant her parents owned. On cold days, he'd carry wood in for them and won the whole family over.

On occasion, "CCC boys had some conflicts in town with local boys with girlfriends who danced with us," explained Frank Munger. Waldo "Red" Fisher admitted to some rivalry between the two groups. "If we chased local girls too much, local boys got upset."

The Corps decided to remedy the situation by holding dances at the camp sites.

"Two or three weeks before you left camp, the Cs organized a dance that was advertised in town. Girls, and their parents as chaperones, were brought in by truck. We never had trouble at the dances at camp, only in the town ones." Michael Rataj

On June 1, 1934, Frank Munger notes in his diary, "They had a dance at Camp Wyman in the day room. There were a lot of girls from Munising there. We had punch and cake and doughnuts for refreshments."

And on June 10, 1934, "We fellows who have been in the CCC a year had our annual picnic in the old campgrounds at Rapid River. We had 32 gallons of beer and lots of girls." Regardless of this writing, Munger was a quiet fellow who preferred to go fishing with his buddies rather than going to town.

Romance flourished among boys and local girls. "Quite a few fellows fell in love and married girls around the camp. The women used to say that 'the CCC men gave women good husbands.'" Michael Rataj

It is true for Robert Fyvie, who met his wife when her cousin helped with the camp's laundry and introduced them. Philipps met his while "he was busy running around Ludington." Cameron Glynn danced with his future bride in a place north of Cadillac.

Years later, Waldo "Red" Fisher and his wife celebrated their fiftieth wedding anniversary at the 1990 MCCC annual reunion.

George Yannett wraps up this chapter with his usual humor. "I liked girls. My mother was one after all."

Going Home on Leave

"I was used to huge barracks, when I walked into my small bedroom at home, I felt claustrophobic." —Leo Lamar Athey

Aside from a few lonely ones, within weeks, recruits began to feel "at home" in camp. The Cs were pretty understanding regarding leaves to go home. Boys applied for a pass and generally got it. Waldo "Red" Fisher obtained compassionate leave for his brother-in-law's funeral. William Tylutki seized every opportunity to go home, but not many others did. Money was short and home was far away.

Camaraderie, a strong sense of allegiance, and identification with the Corps satisfied their need to belong. Besides, only the lucky ones had a warm and comfortable home to go back to. Cameron Glynn hitchhiked home and back until the sergeant told him, "No more hitchhiking! You might get in trouble." Douglas Key Renny also hitchhiked home from Camp Harrison, and his father took him back to Milwaukee Junction to catch a train back. Leo Lamar Athey went back home once, "just got on a train and went; the idea suddenly took me."

courtesy of Douglas Key Renny

Douglas Key Renny on leave, resting at Chandler Park. Note the neatness of his clothes. No wonder mothers and daughters loved CCC boys!

courtesy of Annick Hivert-Carthew

courtesy of Leo Lamar Athey

Boats at Isle Royale waiting to take boys back to the mainland.

"At Christmas, we were given leave to go back to our families. I did not take it." Frank Munger

Back in their own neighborhood, CCC boys impressed their community. "Mothers would see the CCC boys come back, all neat and disciplined, and they signed up their own sons." Michael Rataj

Quite a few refrained from going home for economic reasons. George Yannett's family was so poor, he felt he would be a burden to them; the Corps provided everything he needed.

Families were allowed to visit. Very few did. Money was too tight. Don Ashcroft never went home, but his brother came to visit him, a rare occasion for enrollees.

And then, after six months or the maximum two years in the Cs, came departure day; the final leave.

Going home for good

A few couldn't hack the hard work in the Cs or cope with the surrounding wilderness. They deserted or were let go, but for the average boy, leaving the Cs for good was a heart-breaking experience. Many boys re-enlisted; there were no jobs at home, their family barely survived, and they had formed close relationships. They worked, played ball, ate and slept together. John Selesky and Frank Munger made lifelong friends in the Cs.

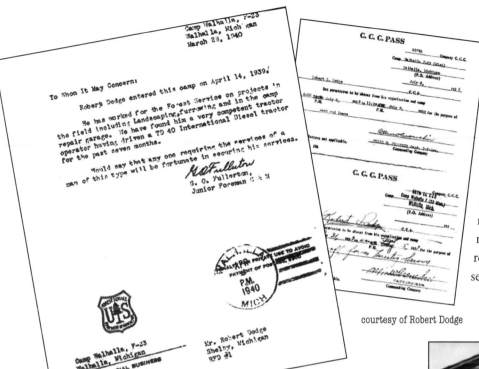

courtesy of Robert Dodge

Boys came a long way in the CCC. At the end of their service, leaders did not hesitate to write meaningful letters of recommendation to secure a job.

courtesy of Robert Dodge

Inevitably, the last day came. Reverend William Elum mentioned he "hated leaving." Years later, Michael Rataj emotionally recalled his feelings. "I was two years at the same camp and had a hard time leaving my friends. The CCC had become my 'home.' Going to my real home was not my home; the CCC was. It was a wrenching experience. I had felt safe at camp; had plenty of food, no war, no problems, and a good job. It was a bit like being inside a cocoon. I had learned good work ethics, to always do the best I could."

Desperate boys sometimes managed to trick the system and extend their stay in the Cs. Wayne Hamilton "left the CCC and weaseled my way back in by lying, and stayed over the two-year limit."

Sooner or later, even "tricksters" were on their own.

Robert Dodge on his barrack's steps.
After a while the boys became a family; leaving the tight group for good was a painful experience.

courtesy of Robert Dodge

Turning boys into men, the CCC's lessons

At an educational CCC conference in 1939, Lieutenant Colonel Sidney Bingham stated that, "It (CCC) must take the boy, feed, clothe, and care for him as long as he is with us. It must help him in the matter of self-improvement so that he can eventually take his place on even terms with the army of wage earners. It should assist him in obtaining a place of opportunity in that wage-earning throng."[1] Judging by the responses of veterans about character development, education, and social skills acquired while in the Corps, the CCC performed rather well. Their testimonials speak for themselves.

What did they learn in the CCC?

Don Ashcroft, "responsibility."

Leo Lamar Athey, "work ethics."

Marvin Bond, "respect for others, and to keep my nose clean."

Bonner Burton, "an appreciation for different degrees of work and how to transform working under adversarial conditions into a positive experience." Testimonial by his daughter, Rainelle Burton.

Arthur Barnes, "education is important."

James Chester Underhill, "an appreciation for the outdoors." Testimonial by his daughter, Diana Dinverno

Wayne Hamilton, "in the long run, they taught us to do things with our hands; things we had no idea we could do. They taught us how to live."

Ray Larson, "to stand on my word."

Elmer Leach, "prepared me for the Army."

Gerald McNeil, "to get along with people."

Frank Munger, "I matured sooner than those who were not privileged enough to be in the CCC. I became very nationalistic, very proud to be an American."

Gerard Perry, "a lot of confidence. When I became a leader, I found out that I could deal with anybody."

Philipps, "I stayed out of trouble. I was taught not to reach for another guy's throat when you're angry."

"CCC and my uncle were a good match. It gave him a sense of achievement and pride." Testimonial by Anne Thatcher, niece of Wells Hall.

Walter Wildley, "got training from adults about anything I wanted to know."

Many of them burst into a chorus, "being in the Cs was the best time of my life!"

[1] **The Soil Soldiers** by Leslie Alexander Lacy

The Demise of the CCC

"I would have stayed; it was an ideal program for young people." —Edward Hartzell

On June 30, 1942, the Civilian Conservation Corps closed its doors after almost ten years of operation. The CCC owed its demise to three factors: the improved economy, the raging war in Europe and the U.S. forces recruiting young men into their fold, and the program's reputation as a relief agency. The Great Depression ebbing, boys were reluctant to work for a "welfare" program, even though the CCC had attempted to shed this image. It was too late, its identification with welfare was too ingrained in young men's mind to be shaken.

An improved economy meant jobs and decent wages. Families did not depend so much on their sons' salary to survive. Qualified boys left the CCC and went back to better paid jobs. The CCC lowered its age admission and require-ments to keep its mission to rescue land and human re-sources. A different kind of youth slipped in the Corps, less

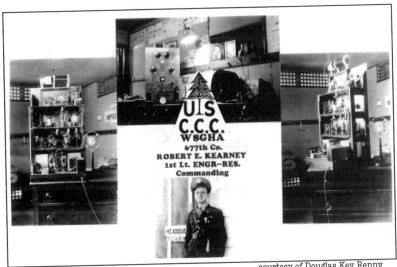

courtesy of Douglas Key Renny

hardy, more immature, and more prone to loneliness and desertion. They were not the majority, but their presence shook up a few camps. Added to this, the armed forces had recalled their most experienced officers from the Cs and replaced them with less qualified ones—an ominous mix. Rebellions and mutinies erupted in several camps in the eastern states and the authority of the officers considerably weakened.

Strangely enough and in spite of these hurdles, the CCC did not lose its popularity among the general population. It continued to benefit many young men and polls showed strong support for the program. The Cs were simply victims of changing times.

Under pressure from Army officials, in 1939, the CCC agreed to become part of the National Defense by preparing the boys for war. It provided twenty hours per week of general defense training. By 1940, all enrollees had to participate in basic army drill, an asset for the many boys who would be drafted or volunteered in the armed forces during WWII.

"Congress wouldn't allocate more money to the CCC because of wartime," says Reverend William Elum. "It was declared defunct by the end of 1942."

Joe Bradish in a radio interview about FDR: "I think it was the most successful program that's ever been presented to the American people. And Roosevelt, you know, he took the initiative. This country was at a standstill. And what he did, he said that he was going to get these kids out into the woods and within, what, about thirty days of his inauguration, he had camps going."

Stan Ward, a hands-on type of fellow, acquired self-confidence and learned how to fix things, especially trucks. According to Edward Hartzell, "The CCC taught me how to get along in the world and go somewhere."

courtesy of Douglas Key Renny

In less than ten years, the CCC had salvaged the American landscape and soil, and re-established the pride of millions of previously untrained, unemployed, and dejected young men. Roosevelt's Civilian Conservation Corps was—and still is—lauded as one of the most important and popular of his programs. The CCC record of accomplishments is outstanding. America owes a great debt to the young men who dedicated their lives to saving the land, heart, and soul of its people for future generations.

Off to War

"CCC men took to war like ducks to water."
—Frank Munger

According to Frank Munger, 80% of CCC veterans joined the armed forces and went to war. "They were disciplined, strong-hearted and used to operating under challenging conditions. My own military career in the Navy was enhanced by my CCC experience."

Reverend William Elum concurred. "CCC boys were renowned to make some of the best servicemen."

While in the Cs Leo Lamar Athey had learned to march and to handle arms with wooden replicas. Athey was "immediately promoted in the Army to Staff Sergeant overseas because of the CCC's excellent preparation." Marvin Bond went right into the Marines where he used his CCC-acquired radio knowledge to his advantage. Robert Fyvie went straight from the CCC into the Marines. Fyvie boxed for exercise in the middleweight category in the Cs. "Boxing 'saved my bones' when I was aboard ship coming back from China during the war. I had learned to drive trucks at camp and was a driving instructor in the Marines at Okinawa."

courtesy of Diana Dinverno

James Chester Underhill
off to war after serving in the CCC

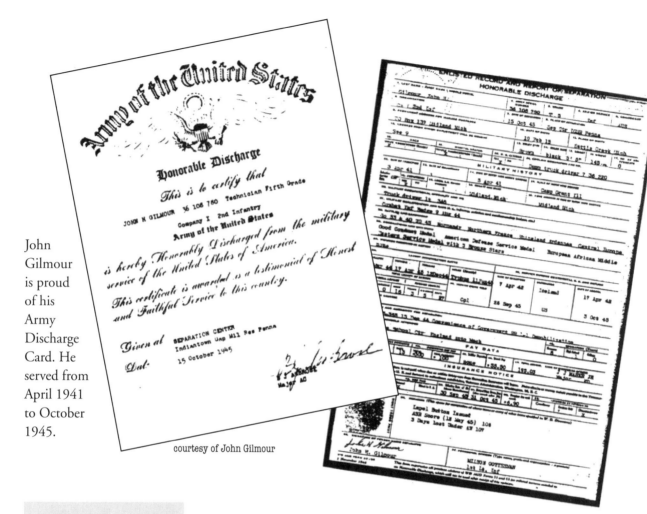

John Gilmour is proud of his Army Discharge Card. He served from April 1941 to October 1945.

courtesy of John Gilmour

Wayne Hamilton joined the Navy in December 1941 and spent five years on a supply ship.

Michael Rataj was sent to the Pacific, the Philippines.

Elmer Leach thanked the CCC for "teaching him to get along with people, a big asset during the war."

John Selesky had learned theory of flight in the Cs and joined the U.S. Army Air Corps where he earned his wings.

George Yannett, an Odawa from the Grand Traverse Band of Chippewa and Ottawa Indians, was sent to Germany and England in 1943. "Europe treated me better than the U.S. If I had the money I'd get back. In England, although I could drive, the Army put me on KP. This when

Philipps was sent all over Europe after D Day. "The Army just gave us one week of training with a rifle and shipped us across the ocean, but I never got to Paris. (Sigh). In London, I was a mail night driver and ran over the curb many times; there were no headlights allowed during the Blitz."

they needed drivers! They were so surprised when they learned I could drive a truck; they'd assumed that I knew nothing."

Alas, wars always bring pain and casualties. Ray Larson sadly stated that, "Many did not come back; it was a terrible war." Michael Rataj and Cameron Glynn lost their friends to WWII.

At the end of the war, the "finest servicemen" returned home, with stellar performances, to reclaim their lives. Judging by the superior quality of the veterans interviewed for this book, the CCC turned outstanding citizens. We, as a people, can be very grateful and proud of them.

Working closely in often dangerous conditions created tight friendships. Here Leo Lamar Athey and Jack Homer drill through red rock.

Although the friendships forged at the CCC were strong, sometimes friends lost touch, according to Michael Rataj. "For a long time I

courtesy of Leo Lamar Athey

did not keep in touch with my comrades, only with Mario, and he was killed in the Pacific. Another mate of mine became a 'big shot.' He did not want to say that he had been in the Cs, and cut off all relations." Rataj was the Roscommon CCC museum docent for many years, entertaining visitors with many fascinating stories.

"I had to melt snow to wash diapers and cook. Clothes froze on the line. There was no water and electricity, no indoor plumbing, just outside toilets. I made little cakes on my two-burner kerosene stove for birthdays. It was rough for me because my father was a professional pharmacist and I was raised in Detroit with all the conveniences of the day. The children were very small and I did not see much of my husband; he worked very long hours. I had to be totally self-reliant and independent." Doris Fedus still shudders at the memory of the day her husband had to shoot a bear to protect the family.

"Bears roamed on the Perch Lake shore, and I was scared to fetch water. One day, a bear came over and my husband had to shoot it. I can still hear the gunshot."

—Doris Fedus

courtesy of Leo Lamar Athey

Although children weren't commonly found at CCC camps, occasionally wives and offspring lived nearby.

courtesy of the FDR Presidential Library

Eleanor Roosevelt in Michigan with Adlai Stevenson and Senator P. McNamara

Women in the CCC

"I was lonely, did not see anybody for days except my husband and children."
—Doris Fedus

The influence of women in the Cs went all the way up to the President's wife, Eleanor Roosevelt, a dedicated proponent of social programs. Mrs. Roosevelt supported the creation of the CCC. Often criticized as First Lady for having strong opinions of her own, Mrs. Roosevelt was a reluctant President's wife and thought it was "hard to remember that I was not just 'Eleanor Roosevelt,' but the 'wife of the President.'"

ER, an enemy of racism and inequality, supported the efforts of Mary McLeod Bethune, the first black person with a high federal position, head of the Office of Minority Affairs at the National Youth Administration to educate and assist young black women.

courtesy of the FDR Presidential Library

A champion of anti-poverty programs, ER, as she signed her letters, fought hard to establish a CCC equivalent program for young women. In spite of her dedication to the cause and the influence she exercised on her husband, the idea of "She-She-She" camps received only tepid support from the administration. A few camps accommodated at most 8,000 women nationwide, none in Michigan. ER frequently visited them. In the photo above, the Roosevelts are visiting a CCC camp in Yosemite, CA.

courtesy of the FDR Presidential Library

ER was very good at rallying fellow women to her causes. She worked closely with good friend Molly Dewson, "America's first female political boss," and ER's replacement as chair of the Women's Division of the Democratic National Committee, to appoint women in influential positions with the New Deal programs to promote economic and work improvement for women. "She-She-She" camps aimed to salvage the self-esteem of women the way the CCC did for the men. Dewson worked on FDR's campaign and FDR respected Dewson's organizational skills and bulldog-like determination so much that he nicknamed her "the little general."

Molly Dewson and ER urged FDR to select Francis Perkins as Secretary of Labor. He did, and she became the first woman to hold this position. As key advisor to the President, Perkins played a vital role in the development of the Civilian Conservation Corps.

Very few women lived in the CCC camps; commandants' wives sometimes lived on-site and occasionally brightened the boys' lives by surprising them with treats. They did not hesitate to coach reading and spelling, and if they had a motherly instinct, it was repeatedly called upon.

Wives of LEMs recruited from far away lived outside of camps, sometimes in tents or trailers pitched in the snow or under stifling heat. Doris Fedus followed her husband to Camps Fox and Newberry. Her husband, Rudolph Fedus, was an unemployed certified teacher who had joined the CCC as an educator. They had three boys in three years and lived in a home-made house trailer near Perch Lake.

Doris met challenges with sturdy equanimity. She used her wits to handle them. "My older boy fell in the lake and I had to 'fish' him out. Another time he swallowed a penny. I bundled the other boys, started our Ford Model A to take him to the camp doctor, but sand trails were snowed in. Somehow he survived."

The wives of local LEMs and leaders fared better; they stayed in their own home and kept their group of friends. They still had to be strong; the job of leader or LEM did not stop at teaching; it involved counseling and looking after the boys' welfare. The men worked long hours.

Laundry women and cooks came daily to the camps. Some of the boys paid to have their pants and shirts pleated according to regulation. It provided the women with a bit of income, and sometimes led to weddings when the women introduced daughters and cousins to the CCC boys.

Local girls, of course, were the biggest attraction. CCC boys were neat, generally good-mannered and danced well—thanks to camp dancing lessons and etiquette manuals. They were hard working and received a small but steady income, two very tangible assets in those desperate times. Boys helped out in the community, charming daughters and their parents. Endearment led to marriage and CCC boys settled in their sweethearts' areas.

In spite of this, the boys' position toward women was ambiguous. They loved their mothers and wrote to them often; they idolized movie stars; and yet could be quite condescending in their vernacular (i.e., "hog-wrestling" for dancing) and attitude with women their age. The National CCC newspaper, *Happy Days*, was rife with jokes about the "She-She-She" camps. It seems to have been a "behind-the-back" sort of behavior, a kind of immature boys' bravado.

Years later, at MCCC reunions, one meets wives of veterans, tagging along with their husbands, smiling congenially and patiently at their husbands' endless exchange of memories. Dorothy Hamilton comments with a grin, "Speaking of women talking and talking, these guys—they'll talk for hours in the rain and snow without noticing it. At the first reunion, in 1986, they had not seen each other in fifty years and were so happy. It went on for hours. It was nice to see them together."

> "Dad talked fondly of the CCC, said that it was a significant part of his life. Mom would roll her eyes every time he mentioned the CCC."
> —Diana Dinverno, testimonial for her father, James Chester Underhill

Mr. and Mrs. John Selesky at the 2005 NACCCA annual reunion at MacMullen Conference Center. Selesky is a CCC alumnus and Golden Glove recipient.

courtesy of the Frank Munger

CHAPTER 29 NACCCA
NATIONAL ASSOC. CCC ALUMNI
Will Celebrate
The 50th ANNIVERSARY of the founding of the
CIVILIAN CONSERVATION CORPS
WITH A
BANQUET
AUGUST 20, 1983 6 P
at
RESERVATION Desired MEIJER BANQUET HALL
2727 WALKER AVE. N.W.
GRAND RAPIDS MI.
Former CCC members families Guests
call
ART BIRD 303 7607
ART DIETRICH 532 9052
HOWARD GILBERT 245 X501
OR WRITE
NACCCA BOX 9338 WYOMIN
Hear again the Music of th

courtesy of Frank Munger

At left: The NACCCA hosted a banquet in honor of the 50th Anniversary of the CCC founding. Former CCC members, families, guests, and interested persons were invited to hear music of the 1930s and reminesce.

Below: A group of alumni posing for future generations. Michael Rataj is in the center. Dorothy Hamilton beams as she explains, "And they talk and talk and talk."

courtesy of Annick Hivert-Carthew

"Our records show that the results achieved in the protection and improvement of our timbered domain, in the arrest of soil wastage, in the development of needed recreational areas, wildlife conservation, and in flood control have been as impressive as the results achieved in the rehabilitation of youth. . .It has been demonstrated that young men can be put to work in our forests, parks, and fields on projects which benefit both the Nation's youth and conservation generally."   —FDR radio address to the CCC in 1936

MCCC Reunions

"I'm still a CCC boy who just grew up. Always a CCC boy; just grew up fast!"
—Walter Wildey

The veterans arrive, some as straight as brooms, others leaning on canes or sitting in wheelchairs. Whatever their physical condition, all display the same pride to have contributed to the CCC's outstanding achievements. Several have never missed a reunion since the first one in 1986; a few are new. Frank Munger happily reports that he's "known some of these fellows for seventy-one years."

Michigan CCC alumni gather every year at a state-wide reunion at the MacMullen Conference Center, Higgins Lake, Roscommon. The MacMullen building serves many purposes, but the CCC reunion is the most appropriate of its uses: a gathering of CCC men in a CCC-built center.

Many veterans are missing; old age and illnesses are taking their toll, or death is keeping them away permanently. Driving long distances has become an issue. The list of those who "Entered Chapter Eternal" grows every year. Those absent are missed, their names are mentioned, a few anecdotes are exchanged.

Arthur Barnes meets fellow alumni in Chapter 163 the first Saturday of every month on the west side of Detroit; they're all from that area and it does not involve too much traveling.

courtesy of Frank Munger

Frank Munger displays his wonderful CCC scrapbook filled with pictures, newspapers articles and official letters.

> "The reasons we put weight on in the camp were discipline, regular meals, study at the same time. We were regimented and felt secure, so we grew up. We had escaped the uncertainty and danger of city life. We could laugh and play in spite of working very hard."
>
> —Michael Rataj

What strikes a visitor the most at a CCC reunion is the friendly atmosphere and the exceptional company. The men breathe honesty, a highly-developed sense of ethics and duty, and good manners. One feels their mental and spiritual strength as well as their no-nonsense approach to life. These men cared and will always care about natural and human resources. They make up the backbone of America and are our inspiration.

The room oozes with the joy of being together. They wear their green CCC caps and clap each other on the back. Rain or shine, they do not care; all that matters is to be "there."

One hears over and over again the same statement phrased in different words. "It was the best time of my life!" and, "I don't want to think what would have happened to me without the Cs." Ray Larson expresses the overall sentiment at the gathering, "I've had a good life and experience in the CCC camp. The Cs helped this country get back on its feet and helped us make it through a very rough time. It was a good thing, and we should have it again."

The reunion usually begins with an opening statement and a prayer by one of the CCC members of the clergy. There are speakers, entertainers and food, but the utmost concern on their minds is kept for last: Bringing back the CCC.

CCC wives know that the Cs were a pivotal part of their spouses' lives and they respect their husbands' happiness. They hear the same stories and jokes year after year, and kindly smile. The pride of the Cs spreads to them.

September 1997: Reunion at Indian Lake

courtesy of Frank Munger

What's Left of the CCC Camps?

"When I was eight, Dad took my whole family back to the U.P. He pointed to some trees, 'See these trees? I planted them.' He was so proud to show us what he'd done."

—Diana Dinverno, testimonial for her father, James Chester Underhill

The CCC legacy stands all around us. Parks, beaches, bridges, trees covering once eroded soil, roads, fire trails and towers, bathhouses and various buildings, fish in rivers and lakes; all are here for our enjoyment. But what happened to the camps after the dissolution of the CCC?

"I took my family back to Isle Royale in the '60s. I thought I'd remember exactly where everything used to be at Camp Rock Harbor. There was nothing left except the 'same' daisies and some chicken-

courtesy of Annick Hivert-Carthew

MacMullen Conference Center, erected by the CCC, and site of the annual Michigan NACCCA reunion.

"I saw CCC boys and WPA workers building check-dams and small ponds and terraces to raise the water table and make it possible for farms and villages to remain in safety where they now are. I saw the harnessing of the turbulent Missouri, a muddy stream, with the topsoil of many states. And I saw barges on new channels carrying produce and freight athwart the Nation."

—FDR's fireside chat, October 12, 1937

courtesy of Annick Hivert-Carthew

A plaque commemmorates the men of the CCC.

A former CCC veteran wrote to Frank Munger, "I believe it is better to build barracks today, than building prisons tomorrow."

coop-like shelters for hikers instead of barracks and tents. I closed my eyes and tried to visualize the way it was, and couldn't." Leo Lamar Athey

Over sixty years have passed since the closure of the CCC. Most of the camps have been dismantled, their sites cleared, and their machinery and memorabilia auctioned off. A simple wooden marker may indicate their former presence, but not always. Nature has taken over. Brush and weeds have conquered truck trails and concrete foundations. No one plays ball in the fields and the laughter of young voices and the commanding tone of older ones have been silent for decades.

In less isolated areas, some buildings have been spared demolition and serve as halls and conference centers, such as the Ludington bathhouse. Many have been revamped and hardly resemble the old edifices.

Abandonment of the camps did not happen immediately after closure of the program. A few served as work camps for conscientious war objectors during WWII. Army troops practiced winter maneuvers in the Western Upper Peninsula sites, and German prisoners of war were housed in former CCC camps Custer and Evelyn, making use of the existing buildings, like the kitchen, infirmary, mess hall, and library. Some of the camps were so remote that no fencing was necessary to avoid escape; prisoners had nowhere to go! A few tried to, but came back, exhausted and demoralized by the insurmountable vastness of the land.

For most veterans, the CCC remains a memory that they love to share. "My uncle waited to have a captive audience, like in a car, to repeat the same stories; the CCC did this and that..." Anne Thatcher, for Wells Hall

courtesy of Douglas Key Renny

Who could escape this wilderness?

CCC Museum, Roscommon, the building where pine cones were tumbled, seeds sifted and dried.

Far right: Periodic newspaper articles remind younger generations of the contributions of the CCC.

courtesy of Annick Hivert-Carthew

50th Birthday for 'Tree Army'
2,500 CCC Veterans Hold Reunion in Wisconsin Forest

courtesy of Frank Munger

"I saw what hard times really were. When we are all gone, no one will understand what hard times really are. There is a big difference between then and now."

—Waldo "Red" Fisher

courtesy of Emily Peck

Installing cedar shakes at Hartwick Pines.

"Some projects were very hard," explains Michelle Kuffer, "especially roofing. We did chain painting, storm cleanup, trail grooming, chain sawing, built boardwalks, trash cleanup, carpentry, picnic tables, safety fire rings, fencing, all of the maintenance at State Parks and forests. We were trained on the job by crew leaders and master carpenters. I enjoyed learning trades, making friends and having fun at the same time."

Robert Brown was very excited to be promoted. "I had my own truck and a tremendous amount of responsibilities. Now, thanks to the CCC skills, I make extra money building chimneys and other structures with cultured stones."

To All Area Citizens

The Michigan Department of Natural Resources cordially invites you to the opening of the new

Michigan Civilian Conservation Corps
Residential Center
CAMP VANDERBILT
Wednesday, August 20, 1986

Opening Ceremony 11:00 a.m.
Tours and Open House 11:00 a.m. ~ 2:00 p.m.

the new center will serve as a base from which young men and women enrolled in the MCCC will live and work on forestry ~ related projects throughout northern Michigan.

rections to Camp Vanderbilt: Go 8 miles st of Vanderbilt on Sturgeon Valley Road. e camp is at the end of the black-top on the rth side of the road near the intersection Sturgeon Valley and Pickeral Lake Roads.

courtesy of Frank Munger

Camp Vanderbilt alumni pose in front of the cabin they restored.

courtesy of Annick Hivert Carthew

Camp Vanderbilt

"At first I just wanted money for college. After a few months it was like a community. I was happy to be away from home, but not in the 'real world' yet."   —Josh Cline

Three Michigan camps were reopened for a few years in the 1980s and '90s—Camp Alberta in the Upper Peninsula, Camp Vanderbilt near Pigeon River State Forest, and Camp Proud Lake near Pontiac. Locating alumni was difficult. Fortunately Josh Cline, from Camp Vanderbilt, responded to the author's appeal on the Internet and was kind enough to stir up enthusiasm from his fellow alumni for this project. This chapter is the result of interviews and meetings with the special young men and women who agreed to participate.

When the MCCC first reopened in the '80s and '90s, it adapted to modern times and became coed. The Army was no longer involved. The MCCC, Americorps, and the DNR banded together to operate the three residential camps.

The original CCC of the 1930s, as we've seen in previous chapters, produced outstanding men; the modern CCC achieved no less with

courtesy of Michelle Kuffer

Painting crew at Waterloo, spring 2000.

courtesy of Emily Peck

Rec hall in the middle with a fleet of vehicles, main office in background. Josh Cline recalls, "We loved to play video games. There were times when a group of us would be playing James Bond on PS2 for days and days on end. When I needed to be on my own, I enjoyed books on the Art of War and listened to the 'best radio station in the state, 94.5 and 95.5—The Zone.'"

"I'd say I was a good kid; my parents might disagree. My hometown had a population of about 2,100 in the middle of few thousand acres of corn. My grandmother knew a girl who was at Camp Vanderbilt and told me about the program. It provided a good salary, some grant money for college, and a place to eat and live cost-free."

—Josh Cline

its men and women. Regardless of its new "management," the MCCC program can still be called "character builders." Camp Vanderbilt alumni display as remarkable qualities as their antecedents. Hard-working, friendly, clear-headed with a highly-developed sense of values and ethics, they form an exceptional group of citizens.

The 1990s girls and boys' reasons for joining did not differ much from the 1930s. Robert Brown, from the Upper Peninsula, wanted to pay back loans from one year in college. He was "feeling lost"—"I still feel lost at times," he grins, and "did not know what to expect in the CCC."

Michelle Kuffer, a city girl from Lansing, was "an athletic youth with no sense of direction at the time." She joined the CCC in 1998 after hearing about it at a mall job fair. She knew that FDR had set it up during the Great Depression to help young men and their families. Michelle intended "to stick to it for only three months, but loved it so much I stayed for the two years allowed." She wants to thank her mother for "suggesting I attend. Without it, I would not have experienced one of the best times of my life. I did not know what to do with my life and was happy to enroll. The CCC/ Americorps booth was the first and only booth I stopped at."

David Turner, a country boy used to hard farm labor, was seeking a summer job. He vaguely understood that the CCC was a state-oriented job. Turner had not left his family before. "I was excited to meet new people and work with them and hopefully acquire new skills for the future."

Timothy Ruhlman liked the outdoors in spite of allergies that bothered him. He took medication rather than leave. Tim grew up on his grandparents' farm and split wood and baled hay for them. In the evening he played cards with his grandma. "I was a quiet and shy teenager who had never been separated from them. My best friend's mom worked for the DNR and told me about this program. The college grant money attracted me. I went for an interview. Two weeks later, they called me, 'bring your stuff'."

Emily Peck drove to Vanderbilt hours after her high school graduation. "I graduated May 29 and packed my car early the next morning to go to Vanderbilt. I knew nothing of the CCC, except I wanted to get out of the house. I read about it in my government class in high school from a poster-size brochure. Free room and board! I had a very sheltered childhood, never participated in sports. My family is very

Enrollees' dorms surrounding courtyard, May 2000. *courtesy of Michelle Kuffer*

Timothy Ruhlman showing off his room. *courtesy of Timothy Ruhlman*

> "We had team 'spirit day.' When everyone got crabby due to bad weather or tiredness, crew leaders came up with group projects to perk us up. We had mini workshops on tractor and chainsaw use and safely. We felt better after one of these."
> —Robert Brown

religious, but they were very supportive. At first I was not interested in the college grant, and then it grew on me. After the Cs, I decided to get a cosmetology diploma. I did and now I am studying to be a physician assistant."

First Impressions

"All the way I wondered what I'd gotten myself into. Once there, I loved being in the middle of nowhere." —Michelle Kuffer

No Army trucks or trains for enrollees of the '90s. They drove to Vanderbilt under their own steam, sometimes alone, sometimes accompanied by a friend or relative.

"Being in 120,000 acres of wilderness was different from being in the country!" says Robert Brown, a native of the Upper Peninsula.

"I drove to Vanderbilt, feeling anxious, as most people would, when going into a job in the middle of the woods. It was an eye opener; rural Ohio does not really provide a multi-cultural experience. Vondre was the first guy I met. He shook my hand and tried to get me to take a puff of his Black and Mild. I had never met or talked to someone who was black before and was not really sure what to make of it. He was a cool guy." Josh Cline

Camp was a ghost town on Sunday; most enrollees went home or visited friends. Those who stayed "hung around." Emily Peck arrived on such a day. "I felt really weird, totally overwhelmed when I turned up. People were sitting around, staring and wondering, 'Who is she? Are

Camp Vanderbilt

courtesy of Timothy Ruhlman

we going to like her?' It was very intimidating. I was very shy and not socialized at all. But everybody was so friendly, outgoing and helpful."

Timothy Ruhlman was apprehensive in case "the group was composed of church fanatics or vagabonds." It was not like that at all. "The ranger took me to the dorm, where I received a warm welcome from other enrollees. Later, I discovered that quite a few of us had been anxious to leave home."

High expectations can let one down. David Turner had expected the place "to be nicer than it was, but people were friendly and the atmosphere fun."

courtesy of Timothy Ruhlman

A Roving Crew Typical Day

"My team and I got to build the sign for my hometown of Tahquamenon Falls. That was exciting!" —Robert Brown

Vanderbilt's roving crew worked four ten-hour days per week. "Roving" means they were assigned to jobs all over Michigan. They had worker's compensation and were paid minimum wage and given an educational grant. If a job was far away, a hotel was paid for and a per diem allocated.

Camp Vanderbilt was assigned the task of building the foundations of the big cedar signs we see at the entrances of state and forest parks. Robert Brown recalls making a sign with stones from Henry Ford's burned summer home and the DNR office sign in Gaylord. However, Robert's eyes twinkle with pride when he mentions, "My team and I built the sign in my hometown of Tahquamenon Falls."

David Turner remembers most "dry-walling, laying wood floors, and heavy concrete work."

Timothy Ruhlman describes one of his favorite jobs.

"Work satisfaction depended on where you were sent that week, what type of work you had to do, and what type of crew members you had. I learned to Mig Weld. I had arc welded when I was in high school but never touched a Mig welder."

—Josh Cline

Josh Cline describes a typical day, a little less regimented than in the "olden times."

6:30 A.M. wake up, get dressed and packed if sent down-state for a week.

Breakfast at the recreation hall

Meeting with our boss telling us specifics on what we're going to do and finding out how we are doing on other projects.

Load into the vehicles and go to location of work. Sometimes we'd be right in camp, other times we'd be all the way to Detroit, Ludington, Bay City.

10 A.M. fifteen-minute break (sometimes longer, depending on how closely we were supervised)

12 A.M. lunch

12:30 back to work

2 P.M. another fifteen-minute break

5:30 P.M leave work or return to camp

Dinner

"The history of every nation is eventually written in the way in which it cares for the soil." —FDR, quoted in Company 696's newspaper, in Wisconsin

"We put a cedar shake roof on one of the historical buildings in Fayette; that was neat. We also built a pole barn and a parking lot at Silver Lake, picnic shelters in Tawas, and a couple of shelters at Seven Ponds.

"If a job was less than one hour away from camp, we traveled by DNR vans and trucks, and returned every night by five P.M to clean the vans inside out and then eat. If farther than one hour's drive, we stayed at a hotel for a week. Rangers did not stay with us and we partied quite a lot. Partying was okay so long as it did not interfere with work the next day. If you overdid it and were not 'well,' teammates did not mind picking up your slack once, but not twice."

"Hauling seventy-pound bags of shingles up a ladder or dragging brush for ten hours was exhausting. I have a heart condition and was told that at any point in time I could step back from heavy work to take a breather," explains Josh Cline.

Emily Peck installed cedar shakes at Hartwick Pines, did some leaf blowing in Gaylord, remodeled Petoskey Wilderness State Park, and erected the Traverse City State Park fence. She too found roofing the hardest job. "As a girl you really had to prove yourself. You did not always work with the same crew as your friends and couldn't wait to socialize with them in the evening."

Crew Leaders

"When I became a leader, I endeavored to be open to suggestions, to work well with my team and to respect their thoughts and ideas." —Timothy Ruhlman

Crew leaders were selected among outstanding enrollees. They set the tone for their group. Timothy Ruhlman had never worked with twenty-five teammates. Before he advanced to crew leader, Tim worked with a good leader, Dan. "Everyone liked him, he was mellow and easy-going, with a good sense of humor; a good guy to work with, showed you how to do things. When I became a leader, I endeavored to be open to suggestions, to work well with my team. I told them: this is what needs to be done. I don't care who does it so long it gets done. People would fall into their own places. "

courtesy of Michelle Kuffer

Michelle Kuffer hugging crew leader Paul as she prepares to leave camp.

Leaders earned $6 per hour, 85 cents more that the regular crew. Josh Cline did not hesitate to accept the post of barrack leader because he "enjoyed the extra money."

Michelle Kuffer was inspired by the leaders. "As a group, we respected each other and generally got on well with crew leaders, and carpenters and managers." Only two leaders gave her some grief, "they were on a 'power trip.'"

A group of Camp Vanderbilt alumni posing in front of the "Upper Cabin," in the Pigeon River Forest. The Vanderbilt crew adopted the cabin and began to refurbish it for their unofficial reunion and hikers seeking refuge. They left a journal for occasional users. One entry says, "Thank you for fixing it. We appreciate it."

courtesy of Michelle Kuffer

Working Together

"I learned to get along with various races and the opposite gender. I understand them better now and look for shared interests in people instead of looking for a person like me." —David Turner

Timothy Ruhlman had never worked with African Americans before. "For the most part, camp was well integrated. At first we had one or two racists, but they soon lost their preconceived ideas. Eventually blacks and whites forged one group."

"It's true," says Emily Peck. "Most of us, blacks and whites, harbored a few prejudices. Blacks from the city expected us to be naïve and a bit thick. They were terrified by wild animals and, of course, we played on that, making up yarns to spook them even more. One African American friend was so scared of bears and all outdoor animals, he'd freak out and not go outside or go camping. On the other hand, most whites were anxious every time someone was said to come from the ghettos; especially I, because in my house no one locked doors. We imagined they'd come with guns and begin shooting. They knew it and played the parts of toughies for the first few days. After a while, we all felt safe at camp."

Play Time

"Girls were pretty outdoorsy. We'd go camping under the stars in the middle of nowhere." —Emily Peck

Enrollees kept their own cars, which gave them the freedom to come and go on and off campus, so long as they were back by midnight on workdays. There was "nothing to do in Vanderbilt, a one-store village." Gaylord and Traverse City were the nearest towns with a slew of distractions, both a long drive from camp.

It is not surprising that during the week, enrollees showered after work, ate as a family, did their laundry in the barracks' washer-dryers, and went into the woods to play. Michelle's eyes shine at the memory. "In my room, I listened to classic rock and country music. At the weekends, we organized trips to Gaylord and Traverse City mall, or went camping and drinking."

"Michelle, Avery and I would jump in a truck and drive until we saw nothing. In winter, we'd play basketball inside Vanderbilt school to get rid of our jitters," adds Robert Brown

Campus was a beehive of activities. Timothy Ruhlman was never lonely. "There were too many people around, I was always invited to do something. We had a TV, VCR, videos and pool tables. No real rivalries, most people had special groups for different activities, fishing, etc. "

David Turner had fun "taping our own 'jackass' videos. Drinking was very much like college. We had camp spirit and spirits!"

Josh Cline talks of drinking more cautiously. "Most people would partake in a drink or two on the weekend, not that we were alcoholics or anything. Sometimes, it was good to have a cold one with your friend and grumble about work."

courtesy of Michelle Kuffer

Boys playing basketball, spring 1999. From left to right: Avery, Chuck, Darren, Adrian, Scott and Will.

courtesy of Timothy Ruhlman

Fishing during their down-time. Michelle Kuffer explains, "When we get together at our 'unofficial' reunions at weekend parties, weddings, camping trips to the Pigeon River State Forest, I feel like the luckiest person alive to have had that opportunity. I'm now a massage therapist in Traverse City. I moved up here from East Lansing to be near my friends. I missed them so much after our camp was destroyed due to budget cuts. I thought we were all forgotten."

> Misbehavior was not taken lightly by management. "The office found out about one raucous party we held in a hotel on an off-site job. They gave us a good chewing."
>
> —Timothy Ruhlman

Discipline

"Absolutely no alcohol, weapons, drugs or pornographic material." —Josh Cline

Crews had a midnight curfew on working days, and no smoking, drinking, weapons or drugs were allowed on campus. Hunting knives and guns could be kept in the office safe. Men and women had different dorms. Camp Vanderbilt had three male and two female dorms with approximately eighteen rooms each. Enrollees had separate rooms. There were also independent male and female leader dorms with three rooms each.

"They were very strict about alcohol. We left campus to drink. I heard of a roving crew who got into trouble with drugs; mine perpetrated only minor infractions." Emily Peck

Conflicts

"We called ourselves 'Big Family.' When we had problems, the 'family' sorted them out. We were like brothers and sisters. Even people who did not like you helped you." —Timothy Ruhlman

courtesy of Michelle Kuffer

Climbing for fun after work. No guys allowed in girls' dorm and vice versa. Emily Peck mentions that "one girl was fired when she sneaked in her boyfriend for the night." Boys and girls mixed in leaders' dorm rooms, where they had more facilities for cooking and fun.

Twenty to forty recruits living and working together in the middle of the woods did not always see eye to eye. "We had some rivalries and there were multiple conflicts. We loved and hated camp, but never really made the separation between the CCC and camp." Josh Cline

Competition between boys and girls over relationships did not exist in the 1930s camps. Boys might have argued over girls, but the girls were from the nearby community, not from camp itself—a big difference. The uneven balance at the modern CCC camps, seven girls for thirty boys, must have made it even more difficult. Michelle Kuffer agrees that "sometimes we had petty disputes over relationships. I did not get along with one girl; just cat-like annoyances from time to time."

Timothy Ruhlman mentions that most people had special groups for different activities—going to the movies, fishing, and hunting.

Payday

"My only regret is to have blown my money away. If only I had matured enough to save!"
—Robert Brown

"I wouldn't trade these memories for all the gold in the world. At our gatherings we reflect and talk about the Cs. I made friends that I'll keep all my life."

—Robert Brown

In exchange for forty hours of work crunched into four days, enrollees received free room and board, worker's compensation, minimum wage and an educational grant prorated to the amount of time they spent in the Cs, again with a maximum of two years.

The crew was paid on Thursday, commonly referred to as "Thirsty Thursdays" by the entire group. "No alcohol was allowed at camp. We went to town to drink or bought beer and drank it around huge campfires in the woods," discloses Michelle Kuffer.

Quite a few, like Robert Brown, regret having blown their money on gas, cigarettes, car parts, and outings. Fortunately, the educational grants were automatically saved for them. Weekend excessive living taught them a lesson. Timothy Ruhlman "has not touched alcohol" since he left camp.

Roofing in Fayette.

courtesy of Timothy Ruhlman

Accidents and Illnesses

No one reported any serious accident or illness, just colds and flu that did not require a visit to the doctor, and the occasional minor cuts and finger hammer-banging while roofing. Josh Cline had a nail shot into his thumb by another fellow and went to the hospital to get a Tetanus shot. Worker's compensation covered job-related injuries. MCCC was very cautious about safety. They held mandatory safety workshops about every machine and occupation.

Camp Vanderbilt did not need a resident doctor or infirmary; enrollees of the 1990s were generally healthy and rarely suffered from the malnutrition and deprivations of the Great Depression. At any rate, they could jump in their own car to go to the doctor or hospital. "Common illnesses were mostly the result of 'Thirsty Thursday.'" Michelle Kuffer

MCCC respected the restrictions of enrollees with special needs, such as Josh Cline's heart condition and Timothy Ruhlman's severe allergies. They could pause when necessary so long as their task was accomplished.

Food

"At the barracks, if the cook was good that day, everyone showed up." —Timothy Ruhlman

After a day's work, the crew was fed a hot meal in the rec room. They ate together, as a family. "Lots of fried food," says Timothy Ruhlman. "I ate so much; I put on over fifty pounds. Now, I've slimmed down, watch what I eat."

Cooks packed cold lunches in deepfreeze coolers and provided propane heaters for hot meals for off-campus day sites. Enrollees took turns cooking. "It

courtesy of Emily Peck

Kelly Carpenter barbecuing pork chops for the crew.

was not a favorite activity," but to the relief of most, one or two recruits loved cooking. When far away on a job and staying at a cheap hotel, each crew member received a per diem allowance for food.

Religion and Spirituality

"The woods were my temple."
—Michelle Kuffer

Each individual was left to look after his/her own spirituality. The Corps was a state-run affair with no religious aspect, but according to Emily Peck, "recruits talked and argued a lot about spirituality. It was a hot topic."

"They let us believe whatever we wanted to believe," says Josh Cline. David Turner remarks that, "We noticed an evolution in our thinking and behavior."

As a group, the CCCs were extremely community-oriented and volunteered to shovel senior citizens' driveways, paint homes, and build playgrounds.

MCCC and the Community

"Camp was located on a former prison camp site. We were guilty by association."
—Emily Peck

By all accounts, recruits of the 1990s had a rougher time with the local community than in the 1930s, although they spent their money there, buying supplies and food, and volunteering on several projects. It seems there was a lot of misconception about MCCC, and most of the young people appear sore about the constant suspicion that surrounded their every move. Maybe, as Em-

"I'll never drink Gatorade again," swears Josh Cline. "We drank so much of it on site; it's put me off for life."

courtesy of Timothy Ruhlman

"One girl, a 'Born Again Christian,' started a Bible study group. Five people signed up, but it fizzled. Religion was mostly a topic of discussion to gain knowledge. We questioned religion and spirituality all the time." Timothy Ruhlman

Sasha the cat—a stray that showed up at camp one day and lived there from 1998-2000. Michelle Kuffer kept her and still has her today. Michelle reflects, "All these dumb reality shows on TV these days, people pretending to have drama, conflict, good times living together, pretending to work hard. We lived the real deal. You put forty kids aged nineteen to twenty-five, mostly men, and a few women, in the middle of nowhere, give them free room and board, make them eat, work and play together and you're gonna have some great stories; too many to tell right now!"

ily Peck says, "The location did it for us. The public at large thought we were prison kids."

"The nearby community was leery of us, thought we were troubled youth." Michelle Kuffer.

"We did not win the community over; our jobs were always 'close enough for government work.'" Josh Cline

"The community around us thought we were mischief-makers, like delinquents. People did not understand the CCC, what it did or stood for. They warmed up a little after a while, when we participated in the Vanderbilt parade and put slides and monkey bars on the school playground." Timothy Ruhlman

"They valued only some of our work." David Turner

In spite of this, many recruits donated their time and energy. Robert Brown explained that, "Kelly organized a volunteer group to shovel old ladies' drives. One night in winter an elderly woman fell sick and if we hadn't cleared her drive that day, the ambulance would never have got in. We did some free roofing and painting."

Here the Vanderbilt crew is doing a free roofing project. "We cleaned up roadsides, power-washed a homeless shelter, and visited old people." Emily Peck

Saying Goodbye to MCCC and Friends

"I was beside myself about leaving. I had settled and felt 'at home,' and it was time to go!
—Robert Brown

1930s and 1990s, different times, same sadness. Leaving the Corps is a traumatic experience. Michelle Kuffer found it "one of the saddest days of my life, leaving the best two years of my life and my best friends behind. I would never have guessed that they'd all be my friends today. In fact, I have very few friends I did not meet through camp."

Emily Peck concludes that "I am 'me' because of the CCC. I am not shy anymore, have learned to be more vocal, stand up for myself and feel confident. I had to cooperate with everyone, even those I did not like.

"One girl always hogged the laundry, left everything in the dryer. One day I took it all out and she wanted me to fold it for her. Before the Cs I would have done it, not any more."

"I stayed two years, as long as we could. I was very sad, like leaving your own family, except it was bigger. Our work was not finished when funds ran out and camp was closed, but we still volunteer to repair things we've built and that are being vandalized."

—Timothy Ruhlman

The unofficial reunions play a big part in former recruits' lives. The camp has been erased. Every summer a group of alumni gather at the former Camp Vanderbilt. They park their cars in a circle, the way the buildings used to stand, and light a fire in the center. "The campfires are the most memorable parts," says Robert Brown. "We had a common bond: everyone was as confused as I was! Former recruits have married each other or got engaged. We have eight couples now."

courtesy of Timothy Ruhlman

The wedding of two CCC alumni: Crystal and Joe Venohr.

courtesy of Timothy Ruhlman

SHOULD MCCC RESIDENTIAL CAMPS BE REOPENED?

We'll leave two alumni to comment: "Hell, yes!"

—Josh Cline

"If I had kids and the CCC was still alive, I'd force them to enroll for their own good."

—Emily Peck

What Did They Learn?

"I am successful today because of the CCC. I have clear ideas and values, am ready for challenges, and have learned to never give up. It prepared me well for college." —Emily Peck

Lesson number one sticking in their memories: You have to work for your money; you must get up and go to earn that paycheck. Yes, it was hard, heavy work. There was much to learn and do, and yet it was "a most positive experience, I would go back in a heartbeat. If they'd kept it open, and I'd been allowed, I would have stayed there forever. Loved it." Emily Peck

Robert Brown and Emily Peck have bought several acres and plan to build their own house from base to top, thanks to the skills they've acquired in the Cs.

Michelle Kuffer felt "well equipped for life after the Cs. I learned about friendship, hard work, teamwork and trust."

David Turner lived "a great experience that I don't regret at all. Not enough people get an experience like that."

The CCC got rid of Timothy Ruhlman's shyness. Josh Cline admits that, "I was not integrated before camp. Also, not being under parental control, I became a little wiser of the ways of life."

These young alumni have grown into adults. They have become America's next human capital, the shapers of our landscape and keepers of down-to-earth values. The MCCC developed their characters and molded them into responsible and dedicated citizens. One feels extremely proud and confident to know that the future of this country is resting in such capable hands.

The New Faces of the MCCC

"I've grown up so much since I have been here." —Jenna McClain, Crew Leader

Hartwick Pines Sign Shop

In Michigan, beautiful cedar signs announce the entrance of state parks and their facilities. Six to eight feet long, sandblasted, painted and erected on solid stone bases, they stand handsomely, impervious to the elements. What many of us do not know is that young hands, hands of teenagers who might not have had a chance to get an education or a job, have fashioned these beautiful pieces of work. They're youths of the twenty-first century, bright and funny. They have stars in their eyes and a strong sense of survival. They love loud music and good laughs. They're the twenty-first century CCC.

courtesy of Annick Hivert-Carthew

Jennifer Failing and Mary Racine holding wood for Jenna McClain. "On the whole, we're friends with everybody; people have their moods, but we manage to get along," comment Jennifer Failing and her coworker Mary Racine, two bright-eyed and small, slim-framed young women who can lift huge six to eight feet long pure cedar signs like seasoned construction workers.

Like many enrollees of the Great Depression and those of the 1980s and 1990s CCC renewal, the sign shop recruits are between the ages of eighteen and twenty-five. They did not know what to do with their lives, how to get an education or a good trade or how to pay for them. Many of them come from poor families, have known hardship and have left home at the average age of eighteen. They've either graduated from high school or are working on their GED with the Cs' help. They work 40-hour weeks, are paid minimum hourly wages ($5.15) with potential raises of $.45 for regular team members and $.90 for crew leaders after 520 hours. They also qualify for educational grants to further their education or pay off previous loans. The longer they stick with the program, with a maximum of two years, the larger the grant is and can be used within seven years of discharge.

They joined the Cs for the same reasons as previous generations: A job to do and money for education.

Jennifer Failing wants to go to massage school, Mary Racine dreams of getting back to study drama as she did in high school, and Jenna McClain will attend art school after she graduates from the program in a few months. The boys, Chris Nelson, Billy Murphy and Alex Chase, have put together a small rock band and are planning to further their education. Billy would like to go back to computer work; Chris to study philosophy and psychology; and Alex visual arts.

This is a new MCCC, one that operates on minimal funds and cannot offer as many of the traditional benefits of former residential camps, where rural and city

courtesy of Annick Hivert-Carthew

MCCC enrollees get time off for job interviews and school training classes. Most stay a year unless they find a better paying job. Robert C. Studer, Camp leader, explains that "there are 'good days and bad days.' Generally, they respect the required code of discipline: Being on time, attendance, no driving/drugs/weapons, profanity, breaks of fifteen minutes, and cooperation. One enrollee was caught stealing and was let go."

courtesy of Annick Hivert-Carthew

Shop sign team. Leader: Robert C. Studer, enrollees: Jenna McClain, Jennifer Failing, Mary Racine, Sarah Jones, Chris Nelson, Billy Murphy and Alex Chase.

The crew is limited to eight members. The present one comprises five women and three men, plus "Bob," their leader. When a young person leaves, he or she is usually replaced by a friend they recommend; very little advertising is required.

males and females of various races and socio-economic strata learned to cohabit and work together in a challenging but safe wilderness environment.

There are no barracks of cabins to live in, no meals provided, and no transportation to get to and from work. Chris Nelson and Billy Murphy share a camper. Two girls live in trailers. Enrollees must drive themselves or carpool to work, which means that most of them come from the Grayling area and are country-bred. They have known each other since high school or earlier, and bring to the sign shop the same friendships and enmities they had formed at an earlier time.

There is no combination of city and rural experiences and hardly any socio-economic blends. They are white with an occasional black teenager. "We had one black recruit, he was local and knew everyone on board. There were no problems," says Robert C. Studer, DNR Camp Leader, a jolly man who is a "father figure" according to the males and "has a good sense of humor and likes a good laugh" according to the females. Everyone agrees he is "fair and understanding; tells us what to do but does not always breathe down our neck."

"We have more of a 'can do it' attitude. We now know what responsibility and work ethics mean. The CCC builds character, develops good self-esteem. You learn that you can survive under any circumstances."

—Mary Racine

Jennifer Failing and Mary Racine sandblasting. Jennifer explains, "Painting is much easier than sandblasting. Sandblasting is by far the most difficult job; it takes such a long time and hurts our lower back and arms. We also lift huge signs of pure cedar." *courtesy of Annick Hivert-Carthew*

"MCCC has taught me so many things! I am living on my own, receive a guaranteed salary, pay bills, bought a car, and learned about schedules. Since I was promoted to crew leader, I have become better at handling people and discovered bad and good things about myself. I know I can handle situations well, sharing and teaching. I have more patience, bite my tongue, put up with different characters, lifestyles, and situations."

—Jenna McClain

"Oh my God, I'm going to hurt myself or get killed!" was the first thought that came to Jennifer's mind when she first saw the huge sandblasting machines and electric saws in the workshop. "I was used to chopping wood with an axe because my dad always wanted boys and he got three daughters, but these machines were something else, very intimidating."

"I was scared too," Mary pipes in, "and now I am so proud of myself. I feel tough, tougher than I thought I was, tougher than the guys working in the sign shop. They have cushy jobs, sticking signs and painting letters."

"Hey, we're not wimps," yells Chris Nelson, defending the honor of the male workers over a radio blasting rock music. "Our job is very repetitive and boring; see if you could stick to it!"

Sarah Jones, a dedicated worker on her way to run some errands, agrees with her female counterparts before leaving. Work is not at all what the girls anticipated. They had to learn the process, step by step; it takes three days to make a sign. "You develop patience because it takes a long time, and we laugh a lot to pass the time." Mary Racine.

Jenna McClain finds it "cool to have hands-on experience. Bob (Robert Studer) gets involved only on big stuff, when machines don't work or need prepping. We work under good conditions. Leaders are understanding, flexible and accommodating.

"I was the first girl to do sandblasting. I had to work two months extra hard, harder than anybody else to become a crew leader. The boys resented it at first. Now, I have an all-girl team working with me; it's not a gender thing, more by affinity.

"Once, I went with the roving crew. It's very different from the sign shop; interesting and fun. I would have liked it, but it meant a drop in pay."

There are no serious accidents, only cuts and bruises; rules and safety are enforced. They wear safety glasses and attend regular training sessions. Mary complains that Jennifer once hit her with a vacuum cleaner by accident, not hard, but it hurt.

The team feels secure in the Grayling area and at work. It may be a "bit boring job and quite repetitive," but it's a reliable source of income. Everyone knows everybody. Moms always know "what they did wrong before they do it."

"We're deep in the woods, but the only animal we see here is the state cop dog." Billy Murphy

"It's a good job. Young people should take advantage of it," says Alex Chase.

Most of these young people have moved out of the family nest. As costs of living keep going up, MCCC pay is not enough to cover all the bills. At the end of a day's work, these boys and girls go home, clean house, talk on the phone, and drive to their second jobs. By all definitions, this is a hard-working group. Their determination to do well is an inspiration to fellow high school graduates and an asset to the DNR and the MCCC.

The spirit of the CCC is not dead, just suffering from financial restraints. Its full force is waiting to be released. The Cs have reclaimed our land and invigorated human resources many times before; why not now?

"MCCC changed what we think of ourselves. We learned to work and live on a schedule, and that we can do more than we thought. It made us feel good. Knowing that we can afford go to school gives us a sense of achievement and of relief," says Jennifer Failing. Mary Racine nods approvingly. "Girls can't rely on marriage; they must stand on their own."

Governor John Engler signing the CCC bill.

Opening Camp Vanderbilt with MCCC carved on a log. Reverend Bill Fraser, Frank Munger, and John Roundtree.

Michigan Civilian Conservation Corps/Michigan's AmeriCorps

GRAND OPENING
CAMP ALBERTA
July 23, 1999

Welcome to the Camp Alberta Grand Opening Ceremony!

10am   Welcome and Introductions
Sue Rose, Camp Manager

Speakers
Paul Tasanovich, Representative, 110th District
Donald Koivisto, Senator, 38th District
K.L. Cool, Director,
Michigan Department of Natural Resources
Rodney Stokes, Chief, Parks and Recreation Division
Sarah Anderson, Camp Alberta Corpsmember,
MCCC/Michigan's AmeriCorps
Reverend William Fraser, CCC Alumnus
Kyle Caldwell, Executive Director,
Michigan Community Services Commission

10:30   Log Cutting Ceremony

11-12   Guided Tours of Camp Alberta

A light buffet luncheon, compliments of Michigan Technological University, is available in the cafeteria ...use.

"We may be knocked down sometimes, but we are never knocked out." —Reverend Bill Fraser, *Thoughts of a CCC Chaplain*, NACCCA Publication

Epilogue

Opening and Closing the CCC in the '80s and '90s

"The need for a conservation corps is as great today as it was in April 1933."
—Senator Daniel Patrick Moynihan

The need for constructive work and positive values had not lessened in the '80s and '90s. Many American youth still fell between the cracks of society. The same social ills of the '30s and '40s followed them; poverty, unemployment, and no support system. Many were raised on and by the "street." They were filled with anger and hopelessness.

These facts did not escape the notice of many CCC veterans. It had worked well before, so why not again? Michigan CCC Alumni formed a committee to re-establish similar programs. They knocked at every political and administrative door until Governors Blanchard and Engler, responding to the committee, opened three Michigan CCC residential camps supervised by the Department of Natural Resources: Alberta in the Upper Peninsula, Vanderbilt at the northern tip of the Lower Peninsula, and Proud Lake in Pontiac.

"My experience in the CCC taught me self-respect, how to interact with those of diverse backgrounds, and even more importantly, discipline."

—Frank Munger

courtesy of Frank Munger

The MCCC admission policy adapted to social and administrative rules of equality. Fifty men and women between the ages of eighteen and twenty-five enrolled in each camp. They were housed, fed, given a uniform, and received training in similar subjects as the "old" CCC; i.e. leadership and construction trades among many others. They were paid every two weeks. Apart from the appeal of working with natural resources, one of the main attractions was a $4,700 education grant from Americorps. The money could be used for college tuition or trade school. In exchange, they agreed to stay in the MCCC for at least a year, and to perform jobs comparable to their older counterparts—moving bears, cleaning up after natural disasters, fire-fighting, planting trees, repairing and updating CCC campgrounds and fire trails.

Politicians come and go, and what a governor agrees to do may not be in the

In his speech at the Governor's Conference, June 14, 1985, alumnus Frank Munger stated, "The Cs gave us a legacy which cannot be ignored, millions of acres of forest, beautiful parks, and miles of roads and trails. . .We cannot thank Representative Mathieu, and all those who supported him, enough, for introducing legislation which brought about the Michigan Civilian Conservation Corps. I wish also to thank Governor Blanchard for his vital support in getting the bill signed into law."

mind of his/her successor. Soon after his election, Governor Engler closed the three camps. Again, a group of veterans, Frank Munger, Bill Fraser, John Roundtree and Dr. Dale Herder worked with Representative Thomas Mathieu to request several meetings in which they convinced the governor of the benefits of CCC residential camps. In December 1993, Governor Engler presented to the committee a check of $20,000,000 to establish the Civilian Conservation Corps Endowment Fund. Interest earned by the endowment can be used to support the Michigan CCC Camps. Even with the help of the endowment, lack of funds forced the closure of Camps Vanderbilt, Alberta, and Proud Lake in 2002.

courtesy of Frank Munger

courtesy of Annick Hivert-Carthew

Statue honoring the men of the CCC in Roscommon, Michigan, the site of the CCC Museum. The Michigan Bring Back the CCC Committee has erected thirty-five statues around the state at the time of this publication.

"I propose to create a civilian conservation corps to be used in simple work, not interfering with normal employment, and confining itself to forestry, the prevention of soil erosion, flood control, and similar projects. I call your attention to the fact that this type of work is of definite practical value, not only through the prevention of great financial loss, but also as a means of creating future national wealth." —President Franklin D. Roosevelt, 1933 Message to Congress

Bibilography & Suggested Reading

The CCC Chronicles, Camp Newspapers of The Civilian Conservation Corps, 1933-1942, Alfred Emile Cornebise, McFarland & Company, Inc., 2004

In the Shadow of the Mountain: The Spirit of the CCC, Edwin G. Hill, Washington University Press, 1990

In the Eye of the Great Depression: New Deal Reporters and the Agony of the American People, John F. Bauman & Thomas H. Coode, Northern Illinois University Press, 1988

The African-American Experience in the Civilian Conservation Corps, Olen Cole, Jr. University Press of Florida, 1999

The Tree Army: A Pictorial History of the Civilian Conservation Corps, 1933-1942, Stan Cohen, Pictorial Histories Publishing Company, 1980-83

Freedom from Fear: The American People in Depression and War, 1929-1945, David Kennedy, Oxford University Press, 1999

The Soil Soldiers: The civilian Conservation Corps in the Great Depression, Leslie Alexander Lacy, Chilton Book Company, 1976

Your CCC. A Handbook for Enrollees. Washington, D.C. Happy Days Publishing Company

We Can Do It! A History of the CCC in Michigan, 1933-1942, Charles A. Symon, RonJon Press, Gladstone, MI

Partner and I: Molly Dewson, Feminism, and New Deal Politics, Susan Ware, Yale University, 1987

Detroit Perspectives, Cross Roads and Turning Points, Wilma Henrickson, Wayne State University Press, 1991

The Roosevelt I Knew, Frances Perkins, 1946

The Presidency of Franklin Delano Roosevelt, George McJimsey, University Press of Kansas, April 2000

Thoughts from a CCC Chaplain, Reverend Bill Fraser, NACCCA Publication

Common Sense Rediscovered, Dale M. Herder, Ph.D.

Madam Secretary, George Martin, New York, Putnam, 1976

Journals and Newspapers

Journals of the NACCCA

"The Civilian Conservation Corps," Patricia Zacharias, *Detroit News*, 12/19/02

"The Brown Bomber—The man behind The Fist," Jenny Nolan, *Detroit News*, 9/29/04

"Brown Bomber" was a hero to all," Larry Schwartz, ESPN.com

"Take the Army out of the CCC," Raymond Gram Swing, *The Nation*

Selection of Enrollees for the Civilian Conservation Corps (Utah), reprinted from First Biennial Report of the Utah State Department of Public Welfare, 1936-38, pp.99-103

State CCC falls on hard times, Dan Sanderson, Record-Eagle staff writer

"Let's all help the youth "aging out" of foster care," Maura D. Corrigan, *Detroit Free Press* 11/15/04

"The CCC and National defense," James J. McEntee, *AMERICAN FORESTS: The Magazine of The American Forestry Association*, Washington D. C. (July 1940)

Happy Days CCC National newspapers, State of Michigan Archives

Internet and Websites

"Roosevelt's Tree Army, Michigan Civilian Conservation Corps," Roger Rosentreter, www.Michigan.gov.home

National Alumni Civilian Conservation Corps Association (NACCCA): For information, research and guidelines, CCC links, museum and CCC store, states listing, and biographies of Alumni.

New Deal and FDR Library websites:

"Letters from the Nation's Clergy"

"My hopes for the CCC," Robert Fechner, Director, The Civilian Conservation Corps

American Forests, "With the Civilian Conservation Corps"

FDR's Fireside Chats

The WPA Federal Theater project, 1935-1939

The Eleanor Roosevelt Papers and Eleanor Roosevelt National Historic Site:

"Anna Eleanor Roosevelt: A Biographical Essay" by Allida M. Black, Ph.D., Mary Jo Binker,

"The Human Rights Years"

"Becoming a Roosevelt"

"ER and New York Politics"

"ER and the New Deal"

"Dear Mrs. Roosevelt": Cries for help from the Depression Generation, and the American Youth Crisis of the 1930s

Mary McLeod Bethune, biography and papers

Frances Perkins, biography and papers

National Archives:

CCC and the National Park Service

"A Brief History of the Civilian Conservation Corps"

"The Civilian Conservation Corps and the National Park Service, 1933-1942, An Administrative History"

Miscellaneous:

"African Americans' New Deal," New Georgia Encyclopedia website

"African Americans in the CCC, A Negro in the CCC," by Luther C. Wandall, New Deal Document Library www.newdeal.feri.org

"Roosevelt's Tree Army," NACCCA website

"Hiawatha National Forest," USDA Forest Service website

"The Mitten," *Michigan History Magazine* website, 9/15/04

Civilian Conservation Corps Materials, National Park Service History Collection, RG 4

"CCC Camps," www.geo.msu.edu

"The Enduring Legacy," www.tva.gov/heritage/fdr

"The Civilian Conservation Corps: Demonstrating the Value of Soil Conservation," History Articles, Natural Resources Conservation Service (NRCS)

"This Social Security—What is it?" An Address by Mary W. Dewson, before the Women's City Club of Boston, Mass. February 17, 1938. www.ssa.gov/history/dewsonspeech.html

"Mary "Molly" Dewson: Portrait of America's First Woman Political Boss," www.ssa.gov/history/dewsonspeech.html

Site to "Bring Back the CCC":

Bring Back the CCC Petition, www.petitiononline.com/CCC2004/petition.html

DVD and VHS

"Camp Forgotten," documentary by William Jamerson

"The Tree Army" by Stan Cohen

Museum:

CCC Museum: North Higgins Lake State Park, Roscommon, MI 48653, tel: 989-373-3559 or 989-821 6364, www.sos.mi.us/history/history.html,

Located in North Higgins State Park, fifteen miles south of Grayling along Roscommon Rd. Exit from I-75 or US 27

Index

About the Author

Annick Hivert-Carthew is the author of seven internationally published books specializing in the history of Michigan, and a renowned keynote speaker. French-born Hivert-Carthew is a member of the prestigious Detroit Working Writers and the English Royal Society of Authors. Author and her family live in Southeast Michigan. In her spare time Hivert-Carthew rides a BMW motorcycle and talks to her cats.